# (Em)bodying the Word

# Renaissance and Baroque
# Studies and Texts

Eckhard Bernstein
General Editor

Vol. 4

PETER LANG
New York • San Francisco • Bern
Frankfurt am Main • Berlin • Wien • Paris

Catharine Randall Coats

# (Em)bodying the Word

## Textual Resurrections
## in the Martyrological Narratives
## of Foxe, Crespin,
## de Bèze and d'Aubigné

PETER LANG
New York • San Francisco • Bern
Frankfurt am Main • Berlin • Wien • Paris

**Library of Congress Cataloging-in-Publication Data**

BR
1609
.C63
1992

Coats, Catharine Randall
(Em)bodying the word : textual resurrections
in the martyrological narratives of Foxe, Crespin,
de Bèze, and d'Aubigné / Catharine Randall Coats.
p. cm. — (Renaissance and Baroque studies
and texts ; v. 4)
Includes bibliographical references.
1. Martyrologies—History and criticism.
2. Foxe, John, 1516-1587. Actes and monuments.
3. Crespin, Jean, d. 1572. Histoire des martyrs.
4. Aubigné, Agrippa d', 1552-1630. Tragiques.
5. Bèze, Théodore de, 1519-1605. Icones.
6. Narration (Rhetoric)  7. Rhetoric—1500-1800.
I. Title.  II. Series.
BR1609.C63  1992  272'.072—dc20  91-28474
ISBN 0-8204-1724-6  CIP
ISSN 0897-7836


**Die Deutsche Bibliothek-CIP-Einheitsaufnahme**

Coats, Catharine Randall:
(Em)bodying the word : textual resurrections in the
martyrological narratives of Foxe, Crespin, de Bèze
and d'Aubigné / Catharine Randall Coats.—New
York; Berlin; Bern; Frankfurt/M.; Paris; Wien: Lang,
1992
(Renaissance and baroque ; Vol. 4)
ISBN 0-8204-1724-6
NE: GT

The paper in this book meets the guidelines for permanence and
durability of the Committee on Production Guidelines for
Book Longevity of the Council on Library Resources.

© Peter Lang Publishing, Inc., New York 1992

Printed in the United States of America.

# Acknowledgments

Aubigné, Théodore Agrippa d'. *Oeuvres complètes*. Ed. by Henri Weber. Paris: Gallimard, 1969. Reprinted by permission of the publisher. All rights reserved.

Halkin, Leon. "Hagiographie protestante." *Analecta Bollandiana* 68 (1950): 461-62. Reprinted by permission of the publisher. All rights reserved.

Cazelles, Brigitte de. *Le corps de sainteté*. Geneva: Librairie Droz S.A., 1982. Reprinted by permission of the publisher. All rights reserved.

From Scarry, Elaine, ed. *Literature and the Body. Papers from the English Institute*. The Johns Hopkins University Press, Baltimore/London, 1989. All rights reserved.

From White, Helen C., *Tudor Books of Saints and Martyrs*, 1963. Used by permission of The University of Wisconsin Press.

Coats, Catharine Randall, "Reactivating Textual Traces: Martyrs, Memory and the Self in Théodore de Bèze's *Icones* (1561)." *Calviniana II* (1991) reprinted by permission of R.V. Schnucker, Pres., SCJ Pub. Inc. All rights reserved.

Coats, Catharine Randall. "Reconstructing the Textual Body in Jean Crespin's *Histoire des martyrs*". Reprinted from *Renaissance Quarterly*, 44, 1 (Spring, 1991), 62-85, by permission of the Renaissance Society of America.

Brown, Peter. *The Body and Society*. New York: Columbia University Press, 1988. Reprinted by permission of the publisher. All rights reserved.

Bèze, Théodore de. *Icones, les vrais portraits des hommes illustres*. Ed. by Alain Dufour. Geneva: Slatkine Reprints, 1964. Reprinted by permission of the publisher. All rights reserved.

Foucault, Michel. *Discipline and Punish*. English Translation Copyright 1977 by Alan Sheridan. Copyright 1975 by Editions Gallimard.

The third chapter appeared in Renaissance Quarterly, 44, 1, Spring 1991: 62-85 under the same title, and a form of the chapter on de Bèze appeared in *Calviniana II.* ed. W. Fred Graham, under the title "The Flesh Becomes Word: Reformation life-Writing in the Martyrological Narratives of Agrippa d'Aubigné's *Les tragiques*".

The first two chapters of this study were written at the Newberry Library, thanks to their generous assistance in the form of a Fellowship to work with special collections.

I am grateful to Professor Robert Cottrell of The Ohio State University, Professor Eugene Vance of the University of Washington and Professor Clayton Koelb of the University of Chicago for their belief in the project, their encouragement, and their willingness to read parts of the manuscript.

Phyllis Palfy of the Interlibrary Loan Department at the Douglas Library of Rutgers University was tireless in her assistance. Her patience and creativity in tracking down sources is truly commendable.

The Reverend William Russell Coats provided always provocative theological discussion, ever-reliable guidance, and loving support. Sara Shaw Coats provided distraction!

The Randall Foundation graciously provided funding for typesetting of this manuscript.

# Table of Contents

# Introduction

## Hagiographical vs. Martyrological Writing

How does a Protestant text, opposed to the use of imagery as a potential form of idolatry, use images of the bodies of martyrs when composing martyrological narratives? The examination of four Protestant martyrologies, one by an Anglican and three by Calvinists, will show the strategy of textualizing the body, writing it into word rather than displaying it as image. Ultimately, the ability so to manipulate images within the space of the text causes a heightened awareness not only of the divine Word, but also of the writer's personal expression. Authoritative authorship for Protestants thus finds its point of origin in the body of the textual *matière*. The body is the indicator that these works are not only theological, but also literary.

Jean Crespin's *Histoire des martyrs,* unlike the English classic to which it is most frequently compared, John Foxe's *Actes and Monuments of the Martyrs*, has suffered from lack of attention; no critical edition of it has ever been prepared, and its last printing dates from the early nineteenth century. It merits attention both for its extensive theological documentation, but most particularly, as I argue in this study, as a literary document. Its redefinition as a literary work, and not one that serves ecclesiastical purposes alone, occurs in and through an analysis of its focus on the body of the martyr, a concentration that is developed in counter-distinction to the hagiographic treatment of saints' bodies. Crespin uses the text as though it stood, synecdochally, for the fragments of the dismembered body. As he compiles and assembles textual documentation by and about the martyr, he purports to reanimate the body of the martyr in a new, textual form.

Théodore de Bèze's *Icones,* conceived as the supplement to his *Histoire ecclésiastique,* was intended to present portraits to accompany, vivify and render more plausible de Bèze's notion of church history. *Icones,* too, is a martyrological narration, although it has not formerly been placed under this heading.  Its contribution to codifying a Protestant aesthetics is also found in its complex, idiosyncratic treatment of the martyr's body:  here, as a component of what I call an emblematic text.

Agrippa d'Aubigné's *Les tragiques,* while not explicitly or exclusively a tract about martyrs, contains portions which may be considered as martyrological narratives (although, again, previous criticism has not examined them as such).  In every instance he borrows material about the martyrs from Jean Crespin, although he reworks it in his own sense.  D'Aubigné focuses on the body.  Like de Bèze, he is concerned with the relationship between words and image, distinguishing the image as characteristic of hagiographical writing, and privileging the word of the martyr in counter-distinction to hagiographies.  His bodies are sites of inscription, in the Foucauldian sense; this inscription is then, to borrow a term from Derrida, placed "sous rature" in a textual operation that creates a redemptive palimpsest of the body.  It is labelled with condemnation, but written into the history of salvation by God (and d'Aubigné himself).

No one has yet performed a literary reading of these three martyrological accounts.  Nor has any effort been made to ascertain qualitatively the intertextual relationships that exist among these writers.  Yet multiple borrowings and reworkings exist which clarify the distinctions among the writers, as well as elucidating a general model of Calvinist martyrological writing — and Calvinist writing, in general.

Unlike Catholic hagiographical writing which may be characterized by a focus on the image, and the spatial rendering and localization of that image, Calvinist martyrologies are above all typified by an insistence on the word — be it of the martyr, of the author or of God.  They are inherently dialogic, and solicit the reader's active participation in a way that hagiographies deny through their formulaic statements and static representationality. Consequently, an examination of the Calvinist works can tell us much about the status of author and reader as Protestants conceived of them.  In our reading of these texts, we are enjoined always to focus on the body in order to hear the word, rather than to recuperate and safeguard the body as a sacred object of contemplation, as in the hagiographic model.  An effective reading of the Protestant narrative actually replicates the methodology the martyrologists themselves employed. The authorship of the martyrologies is also a significant factor. Crespin hides his authorial assertions under the guise of editor. D'Aubigné's martyrological accounts are submerged in a larger, epic history (and therefore go easily undetected). And de Bèze's *Icones* displays problems of self-definition since the author himself is not quite sure to which generic format his word adheres. Yet all of the three men demonstrate to a greater or lesser degree instances in which they reveal themselves acting within their textual production. And, in all cases, again to varying degrees, each man can be found inscribed *en abyme:* as an image of himself reading, as a self-portrait resembling Christ, as one who respeaks the words of the martyr, as one who enters himself on the heavenly rolls of the elect by writing himself into his martyrology.

### Literary Iconoclasm

All four men were influenced by the work and writings of John Calvin. Calvin addressed the issue of bodies in several tracts, always counselling a movement away from the reliance on bodies as theophanic; he opposed the use of relics (*Des scandales*), advised against worship oriented by or towards images: "Prophets condemn images as substitutes for "books ... visible shapes made for the purpose of representing ... are false and wicked...fictions".[1] Calvin assiduously avoided the use of allegory — symbolic, imaged textual example — in his books and sermons, refusing to comment on the Song of Songs for this very reason. While he did not perceive images as nefarious *in se,* he did adhere to the Old Testament interdiction of the "graven image" representation of God; attempts at representing the divine amounted to a flawed, human encapsulation of the ineffable, and hence constituted a distortion of divine perfection. Calvin states that "the thing forbidden was likeness, whether sculptured or otherwise".[2] In addition, specifically the physical body was rendered extraneous in that Calvinism rejected the need for an intermediary; the Calvinist believer had no need of priest or ritual to assure him of his right standing with God: the text alone — *sola scriptura* — would do this. What was required was the integration of the believer into the

Word: a "textualized body" which would imitate the intimate interweaving of *Logos* and human envelope possessed by the Christ. Calvin finds this tactic foreshadowed in scriptural writing, for he notes in *L'Institution* that, although God had imprinted his image on the world, man nevertheless refused to view it, so God necessarily brought his Word to add to and strengthen that image[3]. The commingling of body and word as employed by the Protestant martyrologists can be seen as consonant with this God-given technique. The reverse is also true: if image or body must be redeemed by the addition of word, so human word or writing is unlicensed without the reference to and inclusion of the Body which speaks and enacts the *Logos,* that of Christ. The resurrection miracle is visible to Christians living after the time of Christ only as a textual reproduction: the resurrection takes place over and over, in and through the scriptural text which reconfigures the Body through the citation of Christ's utterances and the witness of contemporary believers. Thus, (em)bodying the word: putting the word in relation to the body, and permitting the body in a new textual manifestation creates a soteric amalgam reactivated by reading.

It can be seen that, for the Calvinist, salvation occurs through well-directed reading and writing, not viewing. The intensely verbal qualities of these texts is always and everywhere apparent. These moments of self-revelation are not theophanic, God-bearing, unlike hagiographies in which revelations of the saint's autobiography are portrayed. Rather, they are expressions of the redeemed self.

A complicating factor in the study of these martyrologies is one of terminology. For decades of scholarship, it has been customary to conflate the terms "saint" and "martyr". Examples of such confusion can be found in the work of Helen C. White, *Tudor Saints and Martyrs,* otherwise a very helpful study. She states, for instance, that "it seems only logical ... that one of the earliest and most influential of *hagiographic* genres to develop was the address of consolation and encouragement to the faithful in time of persecution. Particularly is this type moving when it emanates from one who is to be a *martyr*.[4] I take exception with the term "hagiographic". A specific term needs to be coined to deal with uniquely martyrological accounts. White conflates the two terms, failing to distinguish between the two distinct types of textual treatment: "But with the expansion of the *martyrology* came also an expansion of its complexities. As the new civilization shaped itself out of the shattering and transmutation of the old, one may say that the resources for the creation of *saints'* legends increased."[5] I hope to elucidate a distinction based not so much on nomenclature but on *function* in a text: two different kinds of writing exist, each theologically determined. While those bodies through which they elaborate their textual projects may share traits in common (a saint may, indeed, also be a martyr), the two different manners of writing about those bodies are formulated in opposition to each other. It therefore becomes impossible to combine the terminologies from the two genres and to speak, as Helen C. White does, of such a hybrid (which I maintain would have been perceived by Protestants as monstrous) as a "martyr's legend."[6] To be a saint, it is not necessary to suffer the torment of a martyr's death, although that often does happen. But, more crucial is the theological perspective informing the written work that seeks to talk about saint or martyr. For, very definitely, even the Anglican Foxe, and certainly the Calvinists Crespin, de Bèze and d'Aubigné, do *not* believe their martyrs are saints in the Catholic sense of holy and intercessory beings. They do not seek to venerate or canonize saints, their bodies, fragments of their bodies, or relics as containers of divine presence. Their works clearly stand apart from hagiographical writing, and should be known as martyrologies. They do not try to compose a portrait of the saint, but instead focus on revivifying the instructive words and deeds of a confessor. The distinction between Catholic and Protestant narrative genres is, therefore, essential, both to their self-perception and to our appraisal of them, and needs to be more firmly delineated.[7] The focus on containment and spatial location of the saint's body, both in life (usually in an enclosed, static area, focusing on prayer, fasting and mortification of the flesh: what Brigitte de Cazelles has called "le portrait du saint ascète, corps immobile"[8]), and in death (in a reliquary, shrine or basilica), is a distinctive feature of hagiographical writing alien to martyrologies. Such spatializing makes of the body an image and an object. Describing the aftermath of the martyrdom of Polycarpe, Eusebius records that "we took away the bones, more precious than jewels, more valuable than gold; we placed them in a fitting *place*."[9]

In the same century (circa 800) in which developed the custom of fragmenting the body of the saint in order to produce numerous relics supposedly containing the same sacred power as the integral body, bodies of the saints began to be incorporated into official and popular piety[10]: "A partir du VIIIe siècle, l'Eglise romaine se départit de sa réserve [envers les hagiographes] et peu à peu les *passiones* furent lus à l'office."[11]    The lives of the saints were entrusted to collections of stories which were now read during the mass.    Thus, the body became an object of cultic manipulation. Such a phenomenon would be unthinkable for iconoclastic Protestants, who rejected the notion of enclosed presence or efficacy. Further typical of the Catholic mentality is the emphasis on the intercessory power of the saint.   The body of the saint is perceived to stand in an intermediate position between man and God.   This bodily positioning is reflected in the use to which the body found in the hagiographies was put.    It, too, stood in an intermediate position as it was recited: "Il me semble que la lecture solennelle de la *Passio* avait sa place marquée dans la messe des catéchumènes entre la lecture de l'Ecriture et le Sermon."[12] Such a text is called a "sacrementaire;" it makes of the body a sacrament, a notion Protestants would find intolerable.[13] Scripture is followed by a narration of the saint's life; the body of the saint stands before the human word.   For Protestants, on the other hand, we shall see that body, word, Scripture were all of a piece, as though they were members in one body.

### The Empowerment to Speak

The martyr is textually reanimated in Protestant martyrological narrations as a body, but above all as a body who is empowered to speak.  His physical presence, the primary factor for Catholics, is only incidental for Protestants.  The martyr is not a zone to dispense power, but rather a person to be *read,* and through reading, to come to know God.  Paradoxically, the hagiographic insistence on the *habeas corpus* precludes a speaking relationship with that body.[14]  "Brigitte Cazelles insiste sur la différence de nature entre le saint et le groupe qui raconte sa vie. Par son refus du corps et de toute vie sociale normale, le saint s'exclut de la communauté et l'extrême vertu dont il fait preuve ne peut en aucun cas constituer un modèle ... le projet n'est pas d'imiter le héros, mais de l'invoquer."[15]

One of the most frequently repeated images in the martyrologies is the torn and bleeding body. This image also recurs in hagiographies, but with a crucial difference. The saint inflicts self-destruction while the martyr suffers the inscription of punishment upon his body from an external source. Foucault states that "it was the task of the guilty man to bear openly his condemnation and the truth of the crime he had committed. His body, displayed, exhibited in procession, tortured, served as the public support of a procedure ... in him, on him, the sentence had to be legible for all ... It made the guilty man the herald of his own condemnation. He was given the task ... of proclaiming it."[16] He is written upon by the indictment of an other (and, subsequently, in the text rewritten, or written over, by the words of the author and of God). Since the Protestants do not accept the human ascription of guilt, they find a way, in their texts, to negate that judgement and to proclaim innocence. They do this through a strategy of superscription. The process of punitive writing yields a product: the martyr's confession. This statement is then recuperated and displayed in the textual archives of Foxe, Crespin and to some degree d'Aubigné and de Bèze. Textual production and proliferation is therefore one of the fundamental themes of Protestant martyrologies.

The image of blood reinforces this point. In *Les reliques des saints: formation coutûmière d'un droit,* Nicole Hermann-Mascard instructs that "l'usage était même dans toutes les églises de recueillir le sang des martyrs avec des linges et des éponges qui étaient ensuite déposés dans leurs sépulchres ou inhumés seuls."[17] But in Protestant accounts, martyrs profligately "prodiguent" their own blood, using it to write their confessions when sufficient ink is lacking. Rather than becoming an object of veneration, blood becomes a tool in a process, and retains a dynamic, productive textual capacity. The site of the enshrined saint's body or blood would be visited, with petitions that miracles might there be worked. The blood of the Protestant martyr, however, transforms itself into a textual miracle. Protestants use, but move beyond, the body to read the word/Word. John Foxe describes the martyr's body as one characterized by the words it utters (and revoices in the text): the speaking body, "whose wounds, yet bleeding before the face of God, cry vengeance."[18] The careful positioning of the body in Foxe's description ("before the face of God') emphasizes not physical presence *in* and *per se,* but rather the transmission of a message through face-to-face, that is, verbal, contact. In another instance, Foxe employs the image of blood which accuses: "when you shall be charged with the blood of many martyrs." (*Actes*, I, xiii) Foxe here uses "with" as a synonym of "by": the blood from the martyr's body is productive of an accusatory verb. For him, as for the Calvinist writers, the body has no significance as a body, but only as speech is choreographed through it.

Hagiographic accounts, as well as Catholic ecclesiology, however, constantly document the need to *see* the body, to display it, to touch it. The term "monstrance' ("montrer") describes this aim: this container was specifically designed to elevate and make available to the eye of the worshipper a holy relic paraded in procession.[19] The humiliating processions through the streets in which the martyr was compelled to participate on his way to execution effect a reversal of the triumphant parade of the saint's body. Similarly, the Catholic obsession with the safeguarding of objects that had come into contact with the body of the saint (such as clothing or jewelry—what Hermann- Mascard terms "reliques réelles non-corporelles" in her morphology of relics[20] ) is paralleled by the degradation ceremonies inflicted on the martyr both before and after death. The martyr, prior to burning, is stripped naked. In the case of those martyrs who had formerly held clerical office, the insignia of his church order are systematically removed and formulae are pronounced to abolish the vestmentary ability henceforth to designate him as a man of the cloth. "[They] proceeded to the degrading (as they call it) of the said Master John Castellane. Thus the said Master Castellane being prepared and made ready for his degradation by the officers of the said bishop, was apparelled in his priestly attire, and afterwards brought forth of the chapel by the priests who were thereunto appointed, without his priestly ornaments upon him; and ... the officers gave him the chalice in his hands with wine and water, also the patine and the host; all which things the said bishop who disgraded him took from him, saying, We take from thee ... all power to offer sacrifice unto God... Moreover, the bishop scraped the nails of both his hands with a piece of glass, saying, By this scraping we take away from thee all power ... to consecrate ... Then he took away the chesille ... and taking away the stole ..." (*Actes, VI, 1*)

Many such figures of reversal acted out upon the body can be found in hagiographies and martyrologies. The two invariably contradict each other, thus spelling out a generic self-distinction.[21] At other times, Calvinist martyrologies can be seen to employ Catholic techniques, but to an entirely different end. It is possible, for instance, to conjecture that Crespin, de Bèze and d'Aubigné are improvising in their texts on the Catholic practice of the *translatio* of the saint's body: "*translatio* [was] the translation or movement of a corpse or lesser relics from one place to another."[22] *Translatio*, of course, possessed a literary connotation since the Middle Ages, the *translatio studii*, whereby a body of learning was communicated from a source to an imitator or a disciple. To the extent that, through the compilation of assorted written documents relevant to the martyr's life and death, de Bèze, d'Aubigné (both to a lesser degree) and certainly Crespin and Foxe are, in some literary sense, conveying metaphoric portions of the martyr's corpse from the varied sites of their final dispersal to the text itself. They do so in order to create a new textual body, but one which defines itself adamantly as an anti-relic.

Stylistically, the two forms of writing are distinct, as well. Sofia Boesch Gajano, in *Agiographia alto-medioevale*, singles out repetition as the literary factor most characteristic of hagiographic writing: "procedimenti degli agiografi, la loro ricerca di un crescendo, la tendenza all'accumulo degli elementi."[23] While de Bèze, Crespin and d'Aubigné describe the tortures of martyrs, and while particularly the latter two make mention of certain body parts, the incantatory, obsessional quality of the hagiographic discussion of the body is not evident. Emphasis on the verb, rather than the noun, on dynamics rather than description, typifies the Protestant martyrology. In addition, despite the emphasis on the body, the hagiographic account tends toward a generalized, faceless body (both of the saint and of the writer): "derrière la voix de l'hagiographe, le visage s'estompe, la personne se fait fuyante, selon une humilité qui s'appelle anonymat,"[24] while, perhaps because of the verbal presentation of the martyrs, many martyrological narratives are highly individualized. Even more significantly for the purposes of devising a Calvinist aesthetics of life-writing, the self of the author of the martyrology is distinct and individual. We shall see how, to varying degrees, Crespin, de Bèze and d'Aubigné use their martyrologies to speak of themselves, as well as the martyrs contained in their texts.

### Seeing the Body or Speaking the Body

In order to fully appreciate both the originality of Calvinist martyrological narratives, as well as the tensions that exist in them in relation to the theological system in which they are inscribed, it is necessary to elaborate the distinction between martyrology, as Protestants conceived of it, and hagiography, a Catholic phenomenon. I argue that within the Protestant martyrologies themselves can be found zones of self-conscious reflections upon the nature and import of writing. Especially prominent is a concern not to emulate Catholic saints' lives. Rather, the project is to carve out a *new* genre clearly distinct from and uncontaminated by its *apparent* model. If the attempt were merely to create yet another cycle of saints' lives, then that would constitute *ipso facto* an endorsement of the Catholic hagiographic writing process and, by extension, possibly of Catholicism itself. Therefore, it is crucial that Calvinist writers of martyrologies set themselves apart, by developing their own methodology (as well as their own themes and obsessions), from their Catholic counterparts. I shall attempt to discern and elucidate those strategies by which a new form of writing, uniquely and militantly Calvinist, came into being.

Saints' lives began to be recorded as early as the fourth century.[25] They were intended in part to provide a popular alternative to Scripture. Although subsequently transcribed, many were at first transmitted orally. They are characterized by a legendary flavor borne out through the proliferation of miraculous occurrences ascribed to the saint. The saint, both alive and dead, was believed to possess efficacy beyond the order of the human. His body acted as a conduit for divine intervention in the world. Ronald Finucane explains the saint's activity by suggesting that especially the integral skeleton" ... emitted a kind of holy radioactivity."[26] Thus, the body of the saint acted in typically Catholic fashion: that is, it was conceived of as an intercessor, an intermediary, a body that joined within itself the otherwise separate realms of the divine and the human. "Le culte des reliques se fonde sur le principe que le contact, l'ingestion, l'usage, la vénération d'une chose ayant fait partie, appartenu ou approché une personne riche en vertu, fait participer aux qualités de cette personne."[27] Thus, when saints' bodies began to be fragmented and distributed all over Europe in the eighth and ninth centuries, the fractured portion of the body was still held to possess the same efficacy as the whole body; in some sense, the fragment recalled the entirety. This will be significant later for our discussion of the ramifications and import of the Catholic insistence on dismembering the bodies of the martyrs.

### Bodily Space and Verbal Time

What is particularly characteristic of the saints' bodies, in contrast to the bodies of Protestant martyrs, is that their bodies are spatialized: they are specifically located. As a result, these bodies and body parts sacralize the site that shelters them. They are both contained and containing: their physical, terrestrial housing protects them, while the sacred aura they emit envelops the space in which they are displayed. In hagiographic writing, in counterdistinction to what I term martyrological writing, space is of the utmost importance. Michel de Certeau underscores the significance of the relationship between saint and space: "l'hagiographie ... assoc[ie] une figure à un lieu ... [elle] se caractérise par une prédominance des précisions de lieu sur les précisions de temps ... elle naît en lieu fondateur et devient lieu liturgique."[28] In Calvinist martyrologies, on the other hand, time—the phenomenon of verbal and intellectual memory—is the predominant trait.

Augustine viewed the bodies of saints as garments which, when death had released the soul, nevertheless retained the form and imprint of the person. "One should not disdain and reject as dishonorable the bodies of the dead, especially those of the upright and faithful, those bodies which the Holy Spirit uses like organs and instruments for good works ... [this is] the garment which retains the very nature of the Man."[29] Saints' bodies therefore came to be seen as something which could be put on; holiness could be enrobed; the faithful worshipper could become draped in the qualities of the saints in a phenomenon of physical overlayering. In addition, both Caroline Walker Bynum and Piero Camporesi[30] have shown that many saints' bodies never rotted; their bodies remained integral and uncorrupted, as though still sustained by life. Thus, the saint's body provided a true, constant fixed point of reference: it was always visually verifiable.

That is one of the key differences between hagiography and martyrology. The former displays an artifact that is meant to be seen, while the latter speaks a word that is meant to be heard. Reading, therefore, necessarily operates very differently in the two types of writing, although this has not formerly been recognized. De Certeau qualifies hagiographic writing as "essentiellement théophanique".[31] The revelation of hagiography is visible, it occurs visually, as the text transforms itself into the body of the saint that it describes. The saint is apprehended through his life, in the body, while in martyrologies the martyr exists through the word, inscribed in the text. The text both recalls the body as a point of origin, and moves beyond it to divine Word. In hagiographies, the body is the final and ultimate resting place, that immutable point to which the believer may always return: "le parcours vise le retour à ce point de départ. L'itinéraire même de l'écriture conduit à la vision de lieu: Lire, c'est aller voir."[32] Protestants are far more restless. The roving bodies to which they refer traverse the texts which respeak their words, verbally haunting them, refusing to stay, to be touched, to be seen, but rather demanding to be heard and understood, a far more abstract process. Martyrologies recall the body and reassemble it textually, only to purposefully disembody it, or rather to body it forth in a new, initially unrecognizable form: as pre-eminent text, as *logos*.

Caroline Walker Bynum's study, *Holy Feast and Holy Fast,* emphasizes the body of the saint in its relationship to nourishment. The saints she examines, nearly all women, refuse nourishment in strange and wonderful ways, using what might be called their "anorexia" not to annihilate the body, as a modern sensibility might construe it, but rather, to create of the body a sacred, emptied space in which divine efficacy might move. Bynum constantly uses the vocabulary of containment. By closing the body to ordinary experience, these women open it completely to divine penetration. Their apparent anorexia is in no way a refusal of feeding, but indeed a choice of a different, celestial manna. Their seeming rejection of the body is instead an intense emphasis and focus on corporality: "imitation meant union — fusion — with that ultimate body which is the body of Christ."[33] The Eucharist is the essential point of reference here, and one which is crucial in ascertaining differences between hagiography and martyrology. De Certeau observes that in hagiography, "l'eucharistie est l'objet privilégié."[34] The fundamental sticking points at issue between Catholics and Calvinists were the authority of the Pope, the availability of Scripture, the relevance of intercession and the nature of the *Corpus Christi*. From this perspective, the mass becomes a metaphor for one's apprehension of Christ. Transsubstantiation, the Catholic belief that the host actually contains the body of Christ, mirrors the phenomenon of Bynum's saints.[35] Their bodies become hosts to display their Lord. Calvinists, by contrast, are what we would term "anorectics" (if we decide to employ such terminology). For it is the Calvinist refusal to view the host as containing the Body that leads to their refusal to frequently communicate, and that ultimately separates body from Word. Calvinist theology held that the body of Christ was present in heaven, and simultaneously, symbolically, in the wafer. Such a perception led to a temporal rather than a spatial understanding of Christ, for Christ could not be physically, spatially, visually, localized, but rather existed on different planes, in different ways, both inside and outside of human time.

In Protestant martyrologies, we shall find an emphasis on the body that equals the insistence with which hagiographers speak of the body, but which uses the body in a much different way. Ultimately, the "anorectic" Protestant refuses to eat the body except as a symbol; the Protestant writer incorporates but does not assimilate or digest the body. Rather, he dissects it and then reintegrates it in a dialectic moment of textual experimentation designed to use the body as the point of departure to exalt the divine Word. John Foxe is particularly helpful in dramatizing the dissimilarity between hagiography and martyrology as regards the absorption/rejection of the body, for his book relies extensively on images. This verbal incorporation is more typically Anglican (a Catholic form) than Protestant. We may use John Foxe as a mid-point between the two religious systems, in that Anglicans may accept the corporeal exhibition of Christ in the wafer, and do not reject images as do iconoclastic Calvinists. Théodore de Bèze's *Icones* will constitute a problematic work in this light for, although a Calvinist work, even more extensively than Foxe his text is scaffolded on images, and seems to require them to exist.

In the *Corps de sainteté*, Brigitte de Cazelles notes that "parler du saint, c'est parler du corps."[36] Protestant martyrologies also speak of the body. However, they use it not as an object or artifact but rather as a temporary zone of transmission. The resuscitated body speaks, and then is made extraneous once the words have been transmitted in the text. The centrality of the body, the determining factor of hagiographies, leads, for Cazelles, to "de[s] signes à décoder ... une certaine 'lecture' du corps ... le corps 'fragmenté' ... une perception du saint par morceaux ... On peut poser trois caractéristiques de l'incarnation narrative du saint: (1) d'abord, une insistante visibilité du corps, un portrait qui vient incarner le désincarné ... (2) une interprétation particulière de l'apparence extérieure ... (3) un goût marqué pour le morcellement corporel."[37]

### Right Reading: The Body of Text and the Body in Text

While hagiographic writing thus turns on the act of reading the body, of reconstituting it in order to see it, to itemize all its parts, to describe its physical features, to experience its weighty reality, martyrological narratives privilege the text itself. The body of the martyr is not the goal of reading. Reading itself thus becomes what is at stake. Seeing is devalued; hearing is privileged. Reading does not describe or portray, as it does in hagiography; instead, reading is dynamic and salvific. The entrance of the reader into a martyrological account activates a drama in which the words of salvation are spoken through, incidentally, the body of the martyr. For martyrologists, then, the body is significant, but not as a place of Presence. Rather, it is an organ of speech, to be acknowledged but ultimately disregarded in favor of the syntax its tongue strings together: the text it creates. The martyrology does not collect remains or remnants (*reliquae*); instead, it recalls citations, in an elaborate process of quoting and remembering that is both intertextual and intratextual.

The nature of the reading process and the activity of the reader is also an important area of divergence to elaborate between hagiographic and martyrological accounts. Readers of hagiographies are asked to participate physically in the texts. Foxe's "crossover" text is instructive here. We shall see that Catholics are always characterized by images of superimposition in d'Aubigné's and Crespin's texts. Here, in this passage from Foxe, a sort of physical overlayering, a productive proximity between sacred sign— manifested substantively— and human recipient, is described. Augustine's view of that which was imbued with the sacred as constituting a type of vestment to be put on may also be recalled. Foxe tells of "the year 1501 ... [when] the Lord began to show in the parts of Germany wonderful tokens, and bloody marks of his passion; as the bloody cross, his nails, spear and crown of thorns which fell from heaven upon the garments and caps of men, and rocks [sic] of women; as you may further read in this history."[38] The supracorporal objects change the recipients into signs of God's will: "By the which tokens the Almighty God, no doubt, presignified what grievous afflictions and bloody persecutions should then begin to ensue." (*Actes,* xxiv) This phenomenon of physical overlayering, of wrapping the human in the divine and cloaking the quotidian with the sacred is a process of describing a state of existence of the body. Here, Foxe is more Catholic than Protestant. The focus is always the body.

D'Aubigné and Crespin will also refer to the bloody lance, the crown of thorns, nails and spear, but they will use the term "insignia:" the divine objects retain their nature, while humans are altered to become symbols and to participate in the divine objects. At the instigation of the Word, human bodies will be surpassed and symbolically transformed. Here, the objects act as stigmata on the bodies. In the Protestant accounts, Christ's stigmata are recalled, their corporality rejected and transformed soterically into symbols for writing.

What is called for is a eucharistic feast: the absorption of the body of the martyr that the text serves up. Ronald Finucane recounts the story of a bishop who, face to face with the body of a saint he venerated, grabbed one of the saint's hands, and ate its fingers. This cannibalistic display highlights a significant reality: eating is the manner of hagiographic reading. Saints' lives are not meant to function as *exempla*. Instead, they are intended to *nourish* (and that term, and variations on it, recur constantly in hagiographies).[39] The text is sacred food. Cazelles observes the same process: "à leur tour devenus corps-*mangieres,* les saints peuvent ... servir d'aliments vivifiants."[40] Peggy Reeves Sanday in *Divine Hunger and Cannibal Monsters* studies ritual cannibalism and describes its purpose: "energy is transmitted directly through the vital essence believed to inhere in human flesh or body parts."[41] Not surprisingly, some Calvinists conceived of Catholics as cannibals. Agrippa d'Aubigné's *Les tragiques* and Jean Crespin's *Histoire des martyrs* both dwell obsessively on this theme. For Protestants, reading can never be eating. The absolute refusal of textual substance as food leads to its transmutation into an abstraction: the word which does not nourish but rather "in-spirits". Reading is not a "taking in," but instead a displaying outwardly of that which already indwells: not Christ's body, but His word and spirit. The text thus becomes, through the remembering of bodies and the re-membering of them, a transcription of the precursor inscription.

In hagiographies, the insistence on the body creates "le langage du corps, topographie de 'trous' et de creux: les orifices (la bouche, l'oeil) et les cavités internes (le ventre, ultérieurement le coeur) ... s'inscrivent dans les dialectiques extérieur-intérieur ou englobant-englobé pour permettre [de] riche[s] entrées et sorties."[42] This topography indeed insists on a recuperable *topos,* a place of recollection in which a body may be found. The hagiographic account thus functions as a sort of secondary shrine. In this way, the hagiographic account may even be considered as potentially extraneous, for it displays within itself the simulachrum of a real body that exists elsewhere in some definable space. It is the representation of a reality, and not the reality itself.

It is perhaps because of this characteristic of mimesis that hagiographic accounts and Catholic writing are excoriated by the Protestants. Description, portrayal and painting are linked with the papacy (even by Foxe and de Bèze, who use images in their texts, although in different ways), while reliance on the Word is privileged. Hagiographic narration is considered not to be a form of writing so much as a portraiture project. Cazelles notes that the body of the saint is always a framed, contained body. The movement and action of the impulsion of the word in Protestant martyrologies is negated by the element of static portrayal in the Catholic text: "le portrait du saint ... [c'est] un corps immobile ... qui prie, jeûne et veille."[43] Martyrologies, on the other hand, attempt to re-member the body in order to employ it as an instrument—once effective, then immediately extraneous—to resuscitate speech. Thus, another factor serving to distinguish between hagiography and martyrology is the treatment of word and image, one that will be particularly salient in the work of Agrippa d'Aubigné and Théodore de Bèze. Hagiographic writing depends first and foremost on the image, to produce a type of writing that is substantified, congealed, embodied—what Protestants would view as an anti-writing, since it does not give priority to speech, but rather to description. For Catholics, "c'est la visibilité concrète de l'écriture,"[44] which is essential.

The martyrological word does not ignore the body. Indeed, it welcomes it—at the inception of its project. But the body that speaks in Protestant martyrologies is a body determined by the recollection of the words it once spoke, the words others spoke about it, the words the author currently speaks about it, and the words the reader will speak about it. It creates not spectacle, but audition. "La manifestation est essentiellement locable, visible et non dicible; elle manque au discours qui la désigne, la fragmente et commente, en une succession de tableaux."[45] The presence of the saint somehow engenders a vexing absence; the body exists as a static object to be displayed. But the potential for dialogue, on the contrary, is a primary consideration in the composition of martyrological accounts.

This is a textual body, one composed not of physical members, but rather of literary fragments: recorded testimonies, recited sermons, recuperated texts. The textual body has recognizable members, just as does the saint's physical body: arms, legs, head, hands and heart are all enumerated incessantly. But their repetition works to a different effect. The saint's body is painted through an impasto of visual elements: "la liste [des membres des corps] est quelque peu répétitive, comme si réitérer les mots ...

engendrait la chose même ... [un] spectacle ... la lecture anatomique projette un corps multipliable ou divisable à l'infini ... le corps fragmenté ... cette dispersion bienfaisante ... un corps décomposable ..."[46] The martyrological use of the body recites body parts only as metaphors for texts: a severed arm, the discovery of a decapitated head, the realignment of finger joints, are placed in parallel construction to portions of texts that are found and integrated into the main text. The recomposition of the martyrs' dismembered corpses acts only as a symbol to spotlight the significance of the project of textual recuperation. Bodies are spoken of as signifiers, not as signifieds. In part, such a presentation may be due to the marginalized nature of the Protestants as deviant, hence persecuted, schismatics. Michel de Certeau suggests that "le 'martyre' prédomine là où la communauté est plus marginale, confrontée à une menace de mort, alors que la 'vertu' [qui typifie le saint] représente une église établie, épiphanie de l'ordre social dans lequel elle s'insert."[47] Hence, the body of the church, a customary metaphor, is one difficult to fully realize in any concrete sense for a dispersed and hunted group of Protestants. Therefore, the members of the body of Christ are referred to in a figurative rather than a literal fashion. The body of Christ himself is perceived symbolically rather than actually, and the body of the martyr (because actual, physical reconstitution is literally impossible) is rehabilitated through narrative, through a memorial actualized by respeaking the (present) words of the (eternally absent) body. Thus, hagiography uses the body to speak about the body (and the relationship of the reader's body to that body: can the reader practice a similar mortification of the flesh? can the reader sufficiently model himself on the saint to produce a purified, ascetic body?). But martyrology uses the body to produce writing. It also uses the body to speak about God anthropomorphically. The aim of the *imitatio Christi* is to fashion a body that will blazon forth the visible likeness of God: "the corporeal parts of God [were] deemed manifold and it [was] ... possible ... to 'read' God in corporeal terms."[48] That writing must reinstate the Word. While hagiography requires a geographical situation, martyrology is atopographical: it is the location of an inscription. No archeological endeavor can prevail in the martyrological text: no body is buried there. Rather, reference to the body in *time,* and the effect of memory, will cause the word to live again in the text.

In the lives of saints, it is the *vita* upon which the author and reader meditate: the portrait of a life, fully lived — although admittedly idiosyncratically and, by modern standards, masochistically — *in* the body. That existence remains as some form of energy, even in the bones of the dead saint. The body of the saint may be dismembered, but this does not negate its effect: dispersal engenders proliferation of zones of holiness rather than dissipation of them. The saint is contained in a place, to which one may make pilgrimage. Once at the holy place, the movement operates from inside out. Power radiates out of the saint's body and out of the site of authorship. In a sense, reading works in hagiographies to imitate such a pilgrimage, as the reader visits the repetition in the text of the holy place. The body is displayed and is intended to be apprehended visually, *as body.*

On the other hand, the martyr's body begins in textual form. A *vita* is not portrayed, but rather *acta* are regenerated. The passive body of the saint is countered by the actions of the martyrs, through their confessing words, in the world. While "chaque vie de saint ... est ... à considérer comme un système qui organise une manifestation,"[49] the account of the martyr impels a *demonstratio,* a rhetorical theater in which qualities of eloquence and persuasion are at a premium. Because it has been utterly annihilated through an act of desecration, it does not, cannot, exist as a body. It is recomposed through reminiscences of the words it once spoke: a collective memory reconstitutes a sort of verbal holograph of the martyr's corpse. Here, the movement is from outside, in. Since the martyr's grave or tomb cannot be visited, since it is nowhere verifiable, no pilgrimage can be made. The journey can only be effected in and through narrative. Rather than going to the saint and being acted upon by some numinous presence, the reader enters *into* the *text* and acts therein. For only by being heard can the word be effective. The martyrology requires the reader's participation to activate it; it does not in itself encapsulate divine presence. It is characterized by its concentration: only the text need be consulted, as opposed to manifold sites of pilgrimage housing the myriad of saints' relics. Only an inner pilgrimage may take place, and nothing will be seen at the end of that progress.

Rather, a word will be heard. The reader is placed in the text and speaks with the textualized body of the martyr. This process functions to counteract the Catholic reliance on mediation; it makes salvation directly accessible to the reader, through reading. There are no places to visit, no holy bodies to touch or to adore. The Protestant phenomenon also is faithful to the format of Scripture: in the beginning was the Word, and the word was made flesh. Christ's body was first a verbal entity, then was recorded in a text, just as the martyrs are recalled in *Icones,* the *Histoire des martyrs* and *Les tragiques.* The textual body, additionally, is like to the resurrected body of Christ, which the Gospels describe as changed, altered and not immediately recognizable. The presence of the absent martyrs can only be perceived through reading their word.

Obviously, the role of the reader is crucial for the articulation of the Protestant writing program. We may generalize and say that the word of the reader constantly overlays the word of the text. It is both an ornament on it, a supplement to it, a gloss of it, as well as a part of it.

The reader herself is incessantly named and solicited by Foxe, de Bèze, Crespin and d'Aubigné. In this manner, she himself becomes an inscription, one that attests to the authenticity of the text through the addition of its signature. Michel Foucault, in *Discipline and Punish,* describes a social and legal system wherein the inscription of a crime was written on the body of a criminal. Here we may see the reverse: the inscription of the reader becomes validation of the entire project. By marking the text with her presence, the reader acts like stigmata on the body of Christ. The necessary wound guarantees His divinity, just as the required presence of the reader beholds the pain and proof of the martyr's testimony. The reader views not the body. Instead, she is instructed and empowered to read the inscription the body displays. Foxe cites the martyr Eulalia who cries, "O Lord! Thou art inscribed upon me!" (*Actes,* 271) These are multiple inscriptions: the martyr's body is written upon by the persecutors; the martyr's body is written upon by the divine Word which cancels the persecutors' indictment; the martyr's body is then incorporated into a new textual production; and the reader's presence acts as a reaction to the textual word. In short, the textual recollection of the martyr's body produces an intertextual dialogue among martyr, God, author, author's self and reader.

### Scripting the Body:  An Example of Martyrology/Hagiography

Théodore de Bèze's *Vie et mort de Jean Calvin*[50] is a valuable document in exemplifying the differences between hagiographical and martyrological writing.  Explicitly identified here in an earlier citation from Helen C. White as a "Protestant hagiography,"it is in fact a prime example of how Calvinist writers sought to reformulate the hagiographic style to emphasize word, rather than body, in their characterization of venerated figures.  While ostensibly a *vita,* it does not conform to traditional hagiographies. As a life-writing, it is profoundly Calvinist (both in derivation and technique).  One of the fundamental attributes of hagiography is the reliance on image, the willingness to accept appearance or surface reality as definitive. Coterminous with this trait is the emphasis on the body. Hagiographies are reliquaries:  within the text, as within the saint's tomb, a body is displayed which is believed numinous:  potent and efficacious by its mere existence.  The saint's life is predominantly glorified in and through the body (although the treatment of the body is usually a negative one):  the ability to withstand torture, abstain from food or sexual activity, the power to enact miracles through touch, all demonstrate that saintliness miraculously inheres corporeally.  The Calvinist life-writing, however, might more precisely be called martyrological. The martyr or confessor is known preeminently through his word or speech: the *logos* is martyrological.  It is this utterance which respeaks the word of Christ; the martyr is made verbally and textually Christiform.  In this regard, the body is essentially extraneous as the emphasis is placed squarely on speech.  The Calvinists, people of the Word and of the Book (which each believer could read for himself in his own tongue) predicate salvation on audition and oral/aural and textual interpretation. They will make no pilgrimages to shrines of sainthood; the only spiritual journey they will undertake will be located in the universe of a text.

De Bèze here self-consciously attempts to carve out a new Calvinist genre, one which will counteract the Catholic dependence on body and image, substituting speech and the word—ultimately revealing the Word—for it. Martyrology, rather than hagiography, is the applicable descriptive term for his endeavor, for in it salvation is elaborated as a textual phenomenon. While de Bèze does not omit portraiture of the physical being of his mentor John Calvin, he always uses body or image only as a tool in the process of the revelation of the word/Word; physicality is in no way truth- bearing in itself. Indeed, early in the *Vie* he conflates Calvin's existence not with mundane occurrences but rather with that of textual production (even the title, beginning with "vie et mort," concludes with a list of the books Calvin wrote: "le catalogue des livres par luy composez.") Calvin is fully himself only if apprehended with, in and through his written *corpus*: "Finalement ce sera aussi pour armer de responce les simples, qui sont abusez par faux rapports, estans trop faciles à croire, et par cela sont destournez de lire les livres de Calvin." (6) Calvin's singularity attests to God's approval of him; in typical Protestant fashion, this election is ordained and represented by texts: "en somme tous verront icy clairement, que la vie d'iceluy monstre que ça esté un personnage que Dieu avoit suscité et *marqué*." (6; my emphasis) The "marque" is analogous to the *poincillon*, the impression made on the printed page. The bypassing of the body is also made pictorially evident on the front page of the *Vie et mort*. It is significant that this illustration is not representational, but rather symbolic: it indicates a series of phrases stopping at physical resemblance. A scaffold is erected. Nearby lies a dead man on the ground. A winged figure stands atop his reclining body. The upward movement, from body to angel, is emphasized and given interpretive direction by the fact that this figure holds a book—be it de Bèze's life of Calvin, or God's holy "roolle," register of salvation. The culminating visual point of the image is the book. In the *incipit* to the text, de Bèze reinforces this motion from body to book through the incorporation of a biblical verse from *Hebrews*: "Ayez souvenance de vos conducteurs." He here suggests that his physical existence is in some measure led or directed by Calvin, in a transumptive act of corporeal surpassing which is recalled in the angels' textual redemption of the prone figure in the illustration. De Bèze's biography will speak for Calvin secondarily; Calvin's texts have already spoken, and still speak, for him (albeit, unlike de

Bèze's text, not *of* him, so that the self may be effaced and full focus be directed to God): "Il est vray que les escrits dudit Calvin, et la reputation qu'il a acquise par l'espace de trente ans en ça ou environ, sont choses qui parlent assez d'elles- mesmes." (5) The memory of Calvin, like his existence during his lifetime, is propagated and maintained through the phenomenon of his articulated or recorded speech.

Calvin's books, and de Bèze's writing, possess a virtually physiological relationship to their authors. De Bèze feels himself so strongly indebted to Calvin that he speaks of the *Vie et mort* as an orphan; its father, recently deceased, was not de Bèze (its actual author), but Calvin (whose life "fathered," or furnished the pretext for, the current text): "Et mesmes maintenant ce commentaire ne sortiroit point sans estre comme couronné de quelque excellente preface, ainsi que les autres. Mais il lui en prend comme aus povres orphelins ... cependent je voy cest orphelin sorti de si bonne maison ... et si fort representant son pere, que sans autre tesmoignage il se rendra soy-mesmes ... tres honorable ... et pourtant aussi ce n'a pas esté mon invention, de le recommander par ce mien tesmoignage (car quel besoin en est-il?) mais plustost de me lamenter avec luy de la mort de celuy qui nous a esté un commun pere ... ce livre et tant d'autres d'avoir été escrits par luy-mesmes." (2) Thus de Bèze renounces authorship, yielding to the authoritative word of his mentor. It is significant that nonetheless de Bèze does not silence himself; rather, he enters into dialogue with the biography ("plustost de me lamenter *avec* luy") as though it resuscitated Calvin himself to speak again with his epigone. The verbal character of the interchange operates a form of textual resurrection. The power of Calvin's word is evident and even more so in that, while it was a Renaissance *topos* to call one's book one's child, it was unusual to abdicate paternity to an other, as de Bèze does here. Fathering here occurs, as in the Bible, through the potency of the word. Indeed, de Bèze explicitly assimilates Calvin's word with that of God; confuting Michel Servet's speech, Calvin's word is conflated with divine speech. "Calvin ne refusa point de conférer avec lui; pour essayer de le reduire, ou bien pour le convaincre et redarguer par la parole de Dieu." (16) Elsewhere, Calvin's word is then assimilated to God's: " ... articles ... adjouste quant et quant à bon escient le vray contrepoison qu'il faut

opposer par la Parole de Dieu à leurs erreurs." (39) It is interesting
that as Calvin's word is grafted onto that of Christ, so de Bèze's
writing becomes increasingly aligned with Calvin's word. Towards
the middle of the *Vie et mort,* de Bèze begins a new technique, that
of inserting entire letters from Calvin's correspondence into the
text of his biography. In the case of Calvin's letter opposing Bolsec
(73-81), it is almost impossible to ascertain whether it is Calvin or
de Bèze who is speaking, since de Bèze has practically eliminated
any delineation between the two. The strategy of incorporating
documentation is very much like that Calvinist technique of writing
martyrologies: Jean Crespin, for instance, creates a volume with
virtually no personal intervention or narrative links, quilted from
extensive disparate pieces of documentation: the fragments of the
(dispersed) martyr's body are in this way (textually) reassembled
through the inclusion of his and others' words.

Calvin himself elaborates a theory of self-definition which
deliberately evacuates the self. As in the image on de Bèze's
frontispiece which specified an upward motion of reading indicated
by the vertical lines of the scaffold leading up from the corpse,
through the angel to the apex of the book, Calvin's bodily posture
forms an arrow directed upward, as do his words: "comme
tousiours il disoit, regardant vers le ciel, Seigneur, jusques à quand?
qui estoit la *sentence* qu'il avoit prinse de long temps pour sa
*devise.*" (109) A device is the combination of motto ("sentence")
and image chosen by an individual to convey his sense of singularity. Here, Calvin, by word and image (his posture) chooses to
subordinate his individuality to God.

The few anecdotes de Bèze recounts of Calvin's life are never
exemplary in the Catholic sense; they do not call for the imitation
or conformation of the worshiper's body to the posture of the saint
(often explicitly physical, as in the case of pilgrims who climbed
myriads of stairs on their knees or who spent hours emulating a
saint who customarily imitated Christ by praying with outstretched
arms). Instead, these narratives show Calvin as one who himself
overrides bodily considerations to concentrate on sense or
meaning: the explanation rather than the illustration. In addition,
the physical imitation of Calvin by others—the readers—is
blocked. The response to Calvin is always one which stresses his
uniqueness: "ainsi Philippe Melancthon entre autres prit [Calvin]

dès lors en *singulière* amitié, qui a toujours duré depuis: et dès lors il l'appeloit ordinairement ... le Theologien, par un *singulier* honneur;" (29) "Calvin ... fut tellement receu de *singulière* affection ... " (31; my emphasis). Because of Calvin's singularity, exemplarity in its usual application—a phenomenon which facilitates the production of representation—is not operative here. De Bèze quotes Calvin's understanding of the ritual of baptism as he had experienced it: "volontiers, je renonce le creme et retien mon Baptesme" (8). That is, the bodily phenomenon of the imposition of the blessed oil is extraneous for him; the purpose of baptism is, through oral vows and promises, to conjoin the believer with Christ in a verbal, rather than a physical, bonding.

Thus, oddly, although the *Vie et mort* is written immediately after the death of Calvin—within a context of acute emotional loss of the body or physical presence—the emphasis lies nevertheless on the persistence of speech rather than corporeal disappearance. What really matters is the possibility of the continued propagation of the faith through the magnifying of the Word. Therefore, de Bèze speaks less of members or body parts, and more of "organes," (incidentally) bodily transmitters of a higher reality: "il l'a aimé et honoré comme un excellent *organe* du Seigneur." (18; my emphasis) Rather than a person, Calvin is one who serves a divine role; he is a tool, a method, a waystage, a technique: "le Seigneur donc voulant deslors se preparer chemin à tant de bien qu'il voulait departir à son Eglise par le *moyen* de Calvin ... " (19). "Moyen" is a term which recurs along with "utile" (37, 46) and "interceder" (38), indicating the purpose to which Calvin's life is to be applied. Indeed, his textual productions seem to possess near-medicinal efficacy: "ceux de la langue francoyse voyans le grand profit que feroyent les sermons de Calvin estans fidelement recueillis et unis par escrit." (47) This is a strange form of biography indeed. In fact, we might say it is *unheimlich*, in the freudian sense: behind the cipher of an historical personage is sensed the existence of an already-known Other: God. Thus traditional biography and hagiography are rendered worthless: since Calvin is already "known" by God, what further need to display the events of his quotidian existence? As de Bèze portrays Calvin, one cannot even be certain that Calvin's life possessed ordinary, human vicissitudes. It was so closely wedded to scriptural word that Calvin's existence was more a matter of an *imitatio*. But this is not the Catholic technique of the *imitatio Christi,* in which conformity to Christ's body (in particular, through meditation on his humility and his agony) were recommended. Instead, we might call Calvin's observance an *imitatio scriptura Christi*. The events of his life are already known, fore-modelled on figures of the Gospel: "car [Calvin] avoit ensuivi l'exemple de saint Paul, en servant à l'Evangile à ses propres cousts et despens." (24)

Elsewhere, Calvin is likened to Moses, the events of his exile and initial rejection by Geneva recalling for de Bèze the Hebrews' failure to heed Moses at first (33). When he is not represented as fulfilling a biblical type (in the same manner that Christ, in an anagogical/typological Christian reading, is believed to fulfill Old Testament prophecies which anticipated him), Calvin is described stereotypically as regards his physical being and actions in the world. Only the description of his verbal or written productions conveys any notion of the individual man.

His body constitutes a zone in which certain functions are performed. As minister, Calvin seems a mechanical amalgam who, like a well-calibrated automaton, can always be counted on to execute established pastoral tasks: "car il preschoit d'ordinaire de deux semaines l'une tous les trois jours: il lisoit chaque semaine trois fois en theologie; il estoit au consistoire le jour ordonné, et faisoit toutes les remonstrances:   tous les vendredis en la conference de l'Ecriture, que nous appelons la *conjugation,* ce qu'il adioustoit apres le proposant, pour la declaration, estoit comme une leçon: il ne defailloit point en la visite des malades ... et aux autres infinis affaires, concernans l'exercice ordinaire de son ministre." (37)  The third- person singular pronoun "il" reduces Calvin to a cipher for stereotyped roles; the incessant use of the comma and semi- colon links his actions in a syntax of performance which, while important to the community of believers, is neverthe- less not utterance.  Mere execution of chores is not enough to convey what de Bèze sees as Calvin's importance as the verbal inaugurator of a textual existence of and in Christ. The repetition of numerals delineating elements of time demonstrates quantity, but not yet quality. Even in his physical activities, the overwhelming majority of his time is devoted to those involving the word. Interaction (*conjugation*: a yoking or joining) with the word is privileged above and beyond the fulfillment of other offices: "*outre* ces travaux ordinaires, il avoit un grand soin des fideles de France ... tant en les enseignant, exhortant, conseillant, et consolant par letters en leurs persecutions" (38). The crowning glory of Calvin's achievement as de Bèze sees it comes at the end of this long enumeration and it, too, is associated with the word: the ultimate event is textual production: "cependant tout cela ne l'empeschoit point qu'encores il ne travaillast en son estude particulier et composast plusieurs beaux livres et fort utiles" (38).

Calvin's significance, de Bèze demonstrates, is historical but especially theological. His efficacy derives from his adherence to, and ability to wield, scriptural word. He defeats adversaries through the power of verbal and written word: "ce malheureux là, ayant esté plusieurs fois abattu par Calvin, tant par escrit que de bouche et puis estant desbarassé de l'Eglise de Dieu, est mort misérablement ... pour servir d'exemple à ceux qui se revoltent de Jesus Christ" (22). The "revolte" from Christ is conflated with the dispute with Calvin.

In order for Calvin's word to be an equivalent of the *Logos,* and for his body to be "cristiforme" in a verbal sense, his body must be traversed and surpassed; it becomes a site for scriptural reworking. At times, his body serves as the pretext for scriptural development. After a serious illness, Calvin's return to church is celebrated by the proclamation of Psalm 30: "Or ce fut une grande joye à toute l'Eglise la premiere fois qu'il monta en chaire pour prescher apres sa maladie. Il me souvient que ce fut un jour de Dimanche, et qu'on chantoit le Pseaume 30, qui estoit bien propre pour rendre actions de graces pour sa convalescence." (103) Calvin also utterly destroys his body in the process of conformity to the Word. His is a self-imposed martyrdom effected through scriptural observance: the body which becomes word, at the expense of the body: "Il estoit aussy assailli des hemorrhoides ... la cause de ceste grande indisposition estoit, qu'en *ne donnant nul repos à son Esprit* il estoit en perpétuelle indigestion à laquelle mesmes il ne pensa jamais." (103; my emphasis) As Calvin's body is progressively afflicted, we see ever more clearly the spirit blazoning forth: "parmi tant de maladies, c'est une chose estrange que ceste vivacité d'Esprit ... il y avoit seulement le mal que le corps ne pouvoit suivre l'esprit." (104) The body begins to be left behind ("trainant toujours son pauvre corps" — 107) as Calvin dies to his physical nature and lives in the Word. His body, while ultimately insignificant, is the source of a provisional focus; it is intimately associated with the beginning moments of writing: "... mettre la main à la plume pour escrire. Mais encore y a-t-il plus grand matière de s'esmerveiller, veu que cependant il n'estoit pas sans quelques grands destourbiers, je laisse ses maladies quasi ordinaires, et aussi qu'il a veu sa femme souvent malade quelques années avant qu'elle mourust, comme outre son enfantement bien dangereux ... l'an 1546 il fut longtemps persecuté des hemorroides ... et un bien mauvais ulcère en ceste partie-là." (44-45) The "accidents" of the body menace potential speech and threaten to distract the would-be writer from his task (just as Calvinists perceived the focus on the self as an obstacle to the apprehension of the divine: "... un tumulte ... des coups ... les troubles ... or tout cela estoit pour le rendre inutile à ses estudes." (45-46) Unlike hagiographic accounts, suffering in the flesh does not seem a conduit to, or an indicator of, sainthood: it emblematizes simply the distortion inherent in the human state: "Il fut assez assailli d'une longue et fascheuse fievre quarte, durant laquelle force luy fut à son grand regret de s'abstenir de lire et de prescher." (87) Only writing or preaching can ameliorate and redeem the status of the body: "à son retour de Zurich il se trouva mal d'une defluxion sur l'espaule, qui le fascha longtemps: sans toutesfois qu'il delaissait aucune partie de son ministere ou de ses escrits." (50) And, in an intimate reversal de Bèze demonstrates that the loss of Calvin's physical presence can be compensated for by the collection of his words (as Christ's assumption was palliated for his followers by the arrival of the Paraclete): " ... tous les sermons ont esté escrits et sont bien enregistréz ... on commença à faire estat de recueillir ses leçons et les escrire ainsi qu'il les prononçoit." (47) Transcribed as he spoke, the rereading of these texts resuscitates Calvin's presence.

The textual *corpus/* reactivated, effective *corps,* is placed in others' path, both as a guide and as an obstacle. De Bèze recounts numerous occasions on which, attempting to magnify the word or to instruct of its mandates, Calvin swears on his body ("il protesta que *sa vie en repondroit,* presentement, plustost que de bailler la cene à ceux à qui elle estoit defendue" — 65; my emphasis); or, contrarily, forces his auditor to focus elsewhere than on his compelling physical entity: "il exhorta le peuple de *ne s'arrêter point à sa personne* mais de bien retenir la parole de Dieu qui leur avoit esté preschée" (66; my emphasis); or, at other times, he privileges his body as custodian of the truthful word, denying access to his body in order to protect that which he guards ("un nommé Mathieu Guibalde, tenant des erreurs de Servet ... en entrant demanda en latin, où est Calvin? tendant la main, comme pour la luy presenter. Mais Calvin ayant respondu, Me voici, ne lui voulut toucher la main, disant, il n'est pas raisonnable que je vous baille la main jusqu'à ce que nous soyons d'accord en la doctrine."—69-70). His body, locus of his writing act, conjoined with the speech there produced, acts to lead, fortify and strengthen ("conduict, fortifié et armé") others: "... jusques au jour de sa mort, pour edifier les siens *par sa bouche et ses escrits,* avec une vie *conforme*" (6; my emphasis). The act of others' reception of his utterances is intensely corporeal, almost culinary, as though, like the image of John eating the scroll on Patmos (*Revelation* 10: 8-11), the texts delivered up by the body were edible, immediately assimilable in a physical sense. Not surprisingly, Calvinist understanding of the eucharistic feast—more symbolic than actual—parallels the image here: no body or sign is eaten; rather a *word* is imparted for digestion: "Calvin fit desdites leçons en sa chambre, à quelque nombre de personnes qui s'y peuvent trouver ... et furent icelles leçons recueillies *de sa bouche* ainsi que les autres." (89; my emphasis) The (textual) feeding of the others (his oral words are digested in a literary way: they are recorded in writing "de sa bouche ainsi que les autres, et comme elles sont imprimées"—89) is paralleled by Calvin's continence; he fasts the entire day, the Word traversing his empty body as through a cleared channel. By extension, if Calvin's embodied texts possess power, the book de Bèze composes about such texts will contain efficacious elements, as well: "je leur ay ici mis par escrit en premier lieu tout nuement et simplement l'histoire de sa vie et de sa mort, desquelles l'une et l'autre leur rafraîchiront quant et quant la memoire de sa doctrine." (4) The constant Calvinist concern to exalt the Word is here apparent. Calvin similarly consciously employs his body, bending its physical frailties to further verbal feats: "Calvin eust une fievre tierce ... la force des frissons le pressant ... il fut contraint finalement de s'excuser [de faire le sermon] ... Pour suppleer au defaut, et afin que l'acte ne demeurast imparfait ... un des autres ... acheva ..." (72) The preoccupation with completion, with the fullness of the word is, in de Bèze's account, typical of Calvin as it was to be of his epigoni. The complete word was a dynamic, efficacious verb constituting an action ("l'acte" mentioned above) in the world.

Calvin's last written piece is his will and testament. It adheres to the pattern of his life. Like him, it is described as "singulier;" like his letters, de Bèze incorporates it as "tesmoignage" into the main narrative; like him, it is both effective and economical in the judicious choice of words ("un testament fort bref, comme il n'a abusé des paroles en tant qu'en luy a esté" – 113); like his sermons and *leçons*, his will is the medium for the manifestation of his faith ("il a parlé comme il a crue" – 113) and its wording possesses an active force ("afin que cet acte demeure à perpétuité" – 113). The will, as described by de Bèze, again recalls the motif of the divine register, the list of the "elect" kept by God: "comme il a pleu à Dieu que quelques testamens de ses plus excellens serviteurs ayent esté enregistrez pour estre perpetuels tesmoignages qu'un mesme Esprit de Dieu les a gouvernez en la vie et en la mort." (113) Most significantly, the will has an autobiographical tenor as if, in the moment of death, Calvin is licensed to evoke briefly the (formerly elided) life of the self. The will is an embedded life-writing within a martyrological narrative that has sought not to speak about the personal, human life. The "testament et dernière volonté de M. Jean Calvin" begins with self-effacement; Calvin describes himself as a poor creature who, before his conversion, had wallowed in an idolatrous morass. Calvin then describes the conversion process. As in the de Bèze narrative which displays Calvin progressively absorbed into God, Calvin then portrays God acting for him, not only on his behalf, but in, through and *as* him (114). Calvin next delineates his own perception of his significance as that of transmitter of the Word: "Je proteste aussi que j'ai tasché selon la mesure de grace qu'il m'avoit donnée, d'enseigner purement sa parole tant en sermons que par escrit, d'exposer fidelement l'Escriture sainte." (115) Finally, oddly, he mandates the posthumous treatment of his body; he desires that it be buried "à la façon accoustumée" – that is, integrally – to await the Resurrection (in which bodies are revived by the Word). The body is again displayed as a theater for the efficacious action of the *Logos*. The final silencing of Calvin's speech repositions him firmly in his physical body: "ayant souvent en sa bouche ces mots du Pseaume 39: je me tay, Seigneur, pource que c'est toy qui l'as fait." (131) Reworking biblical imagery, Calvin explicitly likens the moans produced by his pain, testimony to the submission of the body to God's will, to the murmur of a dove, the Holy Spirit: "une autrefois il disoit du cha. 38 d'Isaie ... je gemi comme la colombe." (131). In a final image of the conformity of the body to the Word, Calvin's stifled speech is nevertheless perpetuated by his evocative face, his "speaking" posture: "l'haleine courte le pressoit ... ses prieres estoyent plustost soupirs que de paroles intelligibles, mais accompagnées d'un tel oeil, et d'une face tellement composée, que le seul regard tesmoignoit de quelle foy et esperance il estoit muni." (134) The body, his final resting place, is evacuated by the word at death, to continue to speak elsewhere: in memory and in his written texts. Thus the Calvinist textual body prevails over the corruptible flesh.

De Bèze concludes the *Vie et mort* with a description of phenomena occurring after Calvin's death, relevant to his body and to the remembrance of him. The significant homological link among all these anecdotes is the interplay between "voir" and "ouyr." People come from far away to "see" Calvin, because they had formerly "heard" him. "Plusieurs desirent de le venir voyr ... Plusieurs desirent de voir encore une fois sa face, comme ne le pouvans laisser ni vif ni mort. Il y avoit aussi plusieurs estrangers venus auparavant de bien loin pour le voir." (135) They perform a sort of pilgrimage, but it is motivated by the word. Once arrived, they undergo a process of reorientation wherein their desire to view the corpse is transformed into the ability to hear again his words through memory and through his texts.

De Bèze expresses the persistent textual traces of Calvin's memory by evoking not the physical materiality or matter of his body, but employing rather the term *matière* ("a matter, thing, an argument or subject to write or discourse"[51]), the substance from which writing takes place. This "matière" furnishes the impetus for speech about God as well as about Calvin as God's agent ("la matière que le personnage a fournie de parler de ses vertus" — 138). The concluding image of the *Vie et mort* is thus one

# Notes

1. John Calvin, *Institution de la religion française*, trans. H. Beveridge, (Eerdmans, 1967), I, 5, 95.

2. Calvin, *Institution*, I, 4, 94.

3. Calvin, *Institution*, I, 3, 66.

4. Helen C. White, *Tudor Saints and Martyrs* (Madison, Wisconsin: University of Wisconsin Press, 1967), 8.

5. *Ibid.,* 22, my emphasis. Many other such instances could be named. We note in Bernard de Gaiffier's article, "De l'usage et de la lecture du martyrologue, témoignages antérieures au XI$^e$ siècle," in *Analecta Bollandiana,* 79 (1961), an attempt to discuss martyrs in terms of space which is a characteristic of hagiographies, while martyrologies insist on time and negate space's importance. He states, "aussi longtemps que le culte des martyrs fut célébré près de la tombe et y conserve des attaches, il n'y eut pas de recueils passionaires." (138)

6. White, *Tudor,* 27.

7. White makes the to my mind unthinkable assertion that Calvinists composed hagiographies. Her statement is not fully developed, and would not stand up to examination if viewed in light of the distinctions I propose to draw between hagiography and martyrology. She says that "the pattern of the Puritan saint's life is already apparent in the life of Calvin, which his great disciple Theodore Beza dated from Geneva." (30) She does not proceed to define this pattern, but the suggestion that such a text would possess characteristics in common with hagiographies, when the entire notion of writing, saturated with an alien religious perspective, instead typifies de Bèze's work. See my Chapter Three on de Bèze's *Icones.*

8. Brigitte de Cazelles, *Le Corps de sainteté* (Geneva: Droz, 1982), 81.

9. Eusebius of Caesarea, *Histoire ecclésiastique,* ed. and trans. G. Batby, v. 9, col. 15, in *Sources chrétiennes*, 55 (Paris, 1952-58), 181.

10. Hermann-Mascard, *Les reliques des saints: Formation coutumiere d'un droit* (Paris: Klinckseick, 1975), 17. "Ce commerce familier avec les saints ... sa raison d'être est l'intercession des saints en faveur des fidèles auprès de Dieu."

11. de Gaiffier, "De l'usage," 141.

12. *Ibid.*, 144.

13. Saints' lives were also read at monastic hours. "L'usage de lire à prime le martyrologue ne paraît pas antérieur au neuvième siècle." V. Leroquais, cited in de Gaiffier, "De l'usage," 50.

14. Brigitte de Cazelles rightly notes that "marque d'une sainte insensibilité chez les martyrs, mais preuve et punition de la culpabilité pour la communauté infernale, la torture est une signature moralisante qui s'inscrit dans le corps" (*Corps de sainteté*, 56). However, she does not extend this observation to include the notion of writing on the body as the instigation of further textual production, as I claim it is in Calvinist martyrologies.

15. Mireille Rosello, "Jésus, Gilles et Jeanne," in *Stanford French Review*, 13, note #8, 92.

16. Michel Foucault, *Discipline and Punish*, trans. Alan Sheridan (New York: Vintage Press, 1979), 43.

17. Hermann-Mascard, 24.

18. John Foxe, *Actes and Monuments of the Christian Martyrs* (New York: AMS Press, 1965), xii. All other references in the text will be to this edition.

19. Hermann-Mascard, 135-6.

20. Hermann-Mascard lists four types of relics: (1) the integral body (2) fragmented body parts (3) "reliques réelles non corporelles," e.g. "une tunique portée par le saint," and (4) "reliques représentatives," e.g. "des fleurs déposées devant la tombe qui sont censées être imbues du pouvoir efficace du saint." 100-101.

21. Catholics sometimes oddly reverse the techniques. The parallels between the methods used in the martyrdoms they inflict on Protestants with the means of preparing a noble or royal deceased body for transportation for burial are striking. It is ironic that the same sanitary measures taken in the latter case are employed to inflict pain in the former instance. "Upon the death of high-ranking dignitaries (and especially when such people died far from their native lands and the places that they had elected for burial) their bodies were disemboweled and severed into pieces which were then cast into boiling water. Then, when the bones were loosened from the flesh, they were sent or carried to the place reserved for interment." In addition, late medieval burial practices permitted burial of different parts in different places for royalty who wished to remain in some fragmented, symbolic, bodily form, in death with each portion of their domain. In 1270, the separate burial of the entrails and heart was promulgated, and the practice of separate burial for the heart, entrails and body first occurred in 1321. (257-8) Paradoxically, it is as an attempt at annihilation or destruction that the Catholics separately bury or destroy Protestant hearts, intestines and body, since, despite the practices of

the nobility, the prevailing popular belief (and papal contention) was that "burial without division was consonant with the resurrection of the body." (242) Elizabeth Brown, "Death and the Human Body in the Later Middle Ages: the Legislation of Boniface VII on the Division of the Corpse," in *Viator,* 12 (1981), 221.

22. Ronald Finucane, *Miracles and Pilgrims: Popular Beliefs in Medieval England* (London: Dent, 1977), 22.

23. Sofia Boesch-Gajano, *Agiographia altomedievale* (Bologna: il Mulino, 1976), 152.

24. de Cazelles, 11.

25. Hermann-Mascard, 101.

26. Finucane, 26.

27. Hermann-Mascard, 11.

28. Michel de Certeau, *L'Ecriture de l'histoire* (Paris: Gallimard, 1975), 277-286.

29. Saint Augustine, *De Civitate Dei,* I, 13, v. 12, col. 27.

30. Piero Camporesi, *La chair impassible* (Paris: Flammarion, 1986).

31. de Certeau, 285.

32. *Ibid.,* 286.

33. Caroline Walker Bynum, *Holy Feast and Holy Fast* (Berkeley, California: University of California Press, 1987), 246.

34. de Certeau, 284.

35. Bynum, 251. "It is taught that, at the central moment of Christian ritual, the moment of consecration, God becomes food-that-is-body. This moment then recapitulates both the Incarnation and the Crucifixion. In becoming flesh, God takes on humanity, and that humanity saves, not by being, but by being broken."

36. de Cazelles, 48.

37. *Ibid.,* 49.

38. For a further discussion of the stigmata phenomenon, see Bynum, *Holy Fast.*

39. de Gaiffier, "De l'usage," 43. The saint's life was supposed to supply physical food. Cassiodorus writes to complain about a hagiography that is not sufficiently developed to provide such nourishment.

40. de Cazelles, 86.

41. Peggy Reeves Sanday, *Divine Hunger and Cannibal Monsters* (Cambridge: Cambridge University Press, 1990), 215.

42. de Certeau, 285.

43. de Cazelles, 51-62.

44. *Ibid.,* 60.

45. *Ibid.,* 199.

46. de Certeau, 286.

47. *Ibid.*

48. Ronald Finucane, *Miracles and Pilgrims*, 23.

49. de Cazelles, 50-75.

50. Théodore de Bèze, *Discours de M. Théodore de Bèze, contenant en bref l'histoire de la vie et mort de Maistre Jean Calvin, avec le testament et derniere volonté dudit Calvin, et le catalogue des livres par luy composez.* (Geneva: Perrin, 1564). All other references will be to this text.

51. Randle Cotgrave, *A Dictionarie of the French and English Tongues.* (London, 1611), "matière."

# John Foxe's *Actes and Monuments*: The Body of the Book as Mediator

John Foxe converted to Protestantism while studying at Oxford, and was ordained an Anglican priest in St. Paul's Cathedral in 1560. It is interesting that he composed the initial compendium of the *Actes and Monuments,* also known as the *Book of Martyrs*, in 1559 in Latin, *prior* to his conversion and subsequent publication of the first English version of the work in 1563. An Anglican apologist, Foxe sought in his book to clearly delineate Protestant and Catholic differences, rewriting history into his theological sense. Nevertheless, having written significant portions of the book while still at least nominally a Catholic, Foxe was considerably influenced by the traditional Catholic format of saints' lives, and retained such reminiscences in the manner in which he closely modelled his collection on the ecclesiastical calendar of saints' days of observance. He actually included such a calendar in the *Actes*.

Foxe is noteworthy in several regards, not least being the literary contribution of the collection. He also carefully establishes the spiritual and theological background and adherence of each martyr he discusses, in a much more scrupulous and detailed fashion than do the other Calvinist martyrologists under consideration. Like the Calvinists, he regards the Protestant church as actually reconstituting the body of the early Christian church, and reverses the Catholic status to make Rome appear the theological interloper. In his presentation of the martyr, Foxe generally conforms to a three-part model. The physical action of the martyr is extolled, along with his heroic endurance in the face of torture. The process of interrogation, or examination of belief, is painstakingly recorded, with the martyr's own words providing the climax of this discussion. The manner of the martyr's death is then evoked in gruesome detail. Biblical references are woven into the fabric of the confessional statement as well as Foxe's narrative. Foxe's *Actes* enjoyed enormous contemporary popularity, perhaps because his style functioned dramatically to show to his reader, as though it were actually present, the suffering body of the martyr, along with the words of inspiration uttered at the time of the martyr's agony. In many respects, Foxe's style reproduces contemporary preaching practice; it is a style designed not so much to be read as to be heard, and indeed transcriptions of Foxe's own sermons, such as "The Sermon of Christ Crucified, "which he preached on Good Friday in 1570, repeat the same themes and exhortations as, and in a similar way to the style of, the *Actes*. For this reason, the *Actes* could often be found chained, along with the (Geneva) Bible, in Anglican churches for perusal by the faithful. The concrete image of conjunction with the Bible is evocative of Foxe's own desire to make his book conform to, and display, Scripture.

### The Anglican Compromise

An instructive figure who stands at the intermediate position between the two poles of hagiography and martyrology is John Foxe and his *Actes and Monuments*. While his accounts certainly seem bloodthirsty and polemic in sufficient degree to convey an anti-Catholic sentiment, that is not in fact wholly the case. Foxe always remained an Anglican, a moderate reformer, in contrast to the Puritan position. He conceived of his book as a form of proselytizing to the benighted and misguided, but potentially recuperable, Catholic brethren: "... but only as tendering the conversion of your soul, as perhaps I may do you any good." (*Actes*, xiii.) Foxe's writing does not totally reject, but rather incorporates quite extensively, elements of the former, while also demonstrating similarities with such explicitly Protestant continental martyrological accounts as those of the Calvinists Théodore de Bèze, Agrippa d'Aubigné and Jean Crespin. Through an examination of the construction and content of the *Actes* we may discern areas of textual indebtedness to hagiography which will enable us to more clearly specify the differences between what I see as the separate genres of hagiography and martyrology. We also find zones of authorial assertion which typify the Protestant martyrological form. John Foxe never totally breaks with the concept of intercession; he conceives of his book as a mediator between God and man. His book itself becomes a form of textual body —a bodying forth of its author's presence — that must be confronted and traversed before the Word is heard in its immediacy.

The *Actes* is a more historical narrative than is either that of de Bèze or d'Aubigné, although Crespin's *Histoire des martyrs* does possess an historical schema. Foxe is careful to contextualize each writing. This methodology duplicates his approach to Scripture: "For the better explanation of which mystery, let us first consider the context of the Scripture; afterwards let us examine, by history and the course of times, the meaning of the same. (V, 724) Like Théodore de Bèze, Foxe defines "martyr" according to its original meaning, that of "witness,"[1] and so incorporates in the martyrological portions of his history men and women who were confessors but who did not die violent deaths for their faith. Foxe's work has both a didactic and a missionary intent. Most apparent in the construction of the *Actes* is the emphasis on the book's role in these two regards. The book is a presence in its own right. Foxe refers to his book incessantly: "this book ... I thought ... best ... both for the utility of the book ..." (VI, 778) His book exists in symbiosis with him, and is the mechanism for his intervention in history. He first composes the book, then adds on to it, making himself an autocommentator: "adding withall in the margin, for the better understanding of the reader, some interpretation." (VI, 728) It is immediately apparent that bodies in the text, as well as the body of the text itself, are unlike those created in and by hagiography, for hagiography aims at displaying immediate, integral presence, while Foxe has already fashioned a complex system of text and metatext that, if it does display a body, certainly displays it on many levels.

### The Intercessory Author

Foxe's own body is a paradoxical intruder in the text for he has already dismissed the need for interpretation: "Note good reader, if Christ be where two or three be gathered in his name, what neede is there of a lieutenant." (VI, 745) Yet he constantly intervenes to address his reader and inflect his reception of the *Actes*: "concerning the story of Wickliff, I trust, gentle reader, it is not only of thy memory concerning what went before," (I, 3); "I cannot but laugh in mind to behold the authors of this story whom

I follow." (I, 3) Foxe's methodology is also somewhat of a puzzle. He grants a great deal of space to the Puritan polemic against the reliance on images, quoting one who rails against the "sinneful and vaine craft of painting, carving or casting and stating that 'if the wonderfull working of God, and the holie living and teaching of Christ, and of his apostles and prophets, were made known to the people by their holie living and true ... these things ... were sufficient bookes and kalendars to know God by ... without any image made with man's hands." (265-66)  Yet Foxe's text is extensively illustrated, progressing from the approximately fifty engravings that accompanied the first impression of the text to hundreds in later editions.  And as Warren Wooden notes in his critical commentary on the *Actes,* "the message of these pictures, closely coordinated with the text, was the central message of the text, accessible to all."[2]

Wooden's conclusion is that Foxe was significantly influenced, despite himself, by the already existing hagiographic model, and so incorporated many of its techniques:  "that the history Foxe actually wrote was a Protestant martyrology, with closer ties to the Catholic tradition of hagiography than its author would admit, an encyclopedia of Protestantism ... an anatomy of persecution ... the attraction of the hagiographic element is enormously strong even when Foxe seeks to resist it."[3] While I concur that Foxe writes a martyrology, I would not ascribe the element of pictorial incorporation to the hagiographic influence.  Rather, in my view, the role of images marks Foxe's Anglican affiliation.  He surely is a Protestant, writing a Protestant martyrology, but he is still determined by Catholic churchmanship:    Anglican ritual and aspects of worship remained much like those of the Catholic church. Foxe agrees in principle with the Puritan quoted above, but in implementation he does resort to imagery.  It is in this way that Foxe provides a good test-case for the Calvinist martyrologies he examines later.  But the bodies he displays in his text, and his manner of talking about the body, are usually more like Protestant martyrology than Catholic hagiography.  The site of authorial ambivalence is not the body or the image, as is the case in *Icones*, but rather the book itself.  The paradigm of the body, as Foxe works with it in the *Actes,* is always, first and foremost, the body of the church.  The torments the martyrs experience are so many tortures inflicted on the mystical body of Christ (rather than the physically-represented human/divine body of Christ displayed in the hagiographies). He writes to describe "the malicious hatred and fury of that serpent against the outward bodies of Christ's poor saints ... to afflict and torment the church outwardly ... not to be restrained with the ceasing of those terrible persecutions of the primitive church." (725)

Foxe treats the bodies of the martyrs in the format of separate case studies, lengthily developed and amply documented, but each of these case studies is linked to the others by the theme of its portrayal of the plight of the church, just as limbs are joined to form a body. He manifests a concern for the individual utterance of the martyr which parallels that of Crespin: "all these things to the intent they may the better appear in his own words, I have thought it good here to translate and exhibit the sermon as it was spoken." (V, 767) Foxe's approach to his text is always self-reflective; he is thoroughly aware of the extent to which he writes himself into his text.   He does not experience authorial ambivalence over his place there, as does de Bèze, nor does he seek to minimize his role, as is the case with Crespin.   In this regard, he resembles d'Aubigné, who creates literature from the theological and historical documentation from which he works. Joan Webber's study, *The Eloquent 'I'*, discusses the distinctions between Anglican and Puritan methods of self-portrayal.   Foxe conforms to the Anglican model, one in which the self is experienced as far less problematic than in the Puritan paradigm. Indeed, for the Anglican, the self is a potential place for the creation of art, while Puritans (and Calvinists) experience the self as an obstacle, even a threat, to the necessary focus on God.   On the other hand, Anglicans, because of "centuries of many-leveled [Catholic] exegesis, [learned how to] write the Bible as they read it, to enter into an 'inventive' relationship with this text.. It is a literary relationship."[4]

Foxe is, of course, always careful to link himself with the legitimacy Christ confers.  He does this so frequently, however, that one is tempted to establish a relationship of identity between him and Christ.  He states, "I will speed myself (Christ willing) to proceed toward the time of John Wickliff and his fellows, taking in the order of years as I go ... " (V, 747); "as I say" (V, 23); "if I should seem to any man ... " (V, 94) The references to himself abound. Their frequent proximity to Christ's name also tends to equate the two in the mind of the reader, granting great powers of authority to Foxe in his creation of the *Actes*. Often the syntax is confused in such manner as to create an apparent symbiosis between Foxe and Christ, or between the martyr and Christ. In the following quotation, it is indeterminate whether the "doctrine" referred to is that of Wycliff or of God. The ascription of personal pronouns is, intentionally or not, unclear: "... the name and doctrine of Wycliff forever ... yet the word of God, and the truth of his doctrine, with the ... success thereof..." (95-96).

Foxe is also concerned to spell out his reader's approach to the text. To constitute normative pointers for reading, "Foxe supplements his textual description ... with marginal glosses like 'Note the quick and joyful death of this blessed martyr.'"5 Such asides to the reader disrupt the narrative flow in order to designate it as story to be evaluated; critical commentary is called for. Foxe often coopts the reader through the use of the first-person plural, placing both himself and the reader in proximity to Christ: "now to thee, (the Lord willing) we will add ..." (V, 728) As the body of the text ranges far and wide to incorporate material, he compels the reader's body to follow suit: " ... to return from whence we digressed..." (v, 800) The *Actes* never appears neutral; it is never unmediated by Foxe. "I ... myself ... also may the better prepare the mind of the reader to the entering of that story." (747) The faithful are asked not to assess from the evidence (as is the case with the *Histoire des martyrs*) or to learn from a composite, emblematic presentation (as de Bèze demands), or to be swayed by the emotion generated in and by the text (as in d'Aubigné's *Tragiques*). Rather, the reader is instructed to accept Foxe's story: "By this, I suppose, may sufficiently appear to the indifferent, the nature and condition of Wycliff, how far it was from the ambition and pride ... How true this is, He only knoweth best, that rightly shall judge in both the one and the other." (800) While *Actes* at first seems a legal document, we see that Christ preempts the final ability to judge; judgement in the text is necessarily deferred. But, as we have noted, Foxe's constant association of himself with Christ relegates the Last Judgement an afterthought: Foxe has already weighed the evidence and written the authoritative opinion. *Actes* in fact is set up as a mediator in history; the book will intervene to reshape history in its own sense. It is definitive and trenchant. Foxe, who appears constantly to digress and elaborate, actually sees himself as mercilessly wielding a scalpel in his text to shave off extraneous material. He refers his reader to other texts to fill in background knowledge in order to be able to devote all his time to shaping his text into a potent vehicle for his argument: "these, because they are impertinent and make too long a digression from the matter of Wickliff, I refer the reader to other histories, such as that of St. Alban's." (804) Thus, not only does Foxe refer always to himself, but also to the reader whom he perceives as an active pupil in the process of textual instruction. Webber has also noted this phenomenon as regards other Anglican writers: "Although he may be full of pretended indifference toward the reader, he is constantly reacting to the reader ... even asking for the reader's cooperation in the writing of his book ... Consciousness of self as subject ... consciousness of self in the eyes of the reader..."[6] Additionally, Foxe engages — not himself, but the reader, through the directions given in the *Actes* — in an intertextual relationship with other works (but always one of a secondary significance, since we note that the reader is sent to read other books which Foxe considers to be less authoritative than his own). The reader is called to be "vigilant" and attentive to the prescriptions and pronouncements of the book: "these are the words of the history; whereby it is evident unto the vigilant reader, unto what grossness the true knowledge of the spiritual doctrine of the gospel had generated." (794) The vigilance of the reader is defined in several ways. As we have seen, the reader takes Foxe's text as normative and definitive. Foxe's method is in contrast to the manner in which Crespin invokes his reader. For, while Foxe constantly adds to his work in subsequent editions, unlike Crespin he does not explicitly solicit the reader's cooperation in submitting further documentation to him for consideration. In this regard, the *Histoire des martyrs* is far more open-ended, a mutual production of Crespin and the reader, while the *Actes* is more directive. Like the process of the canonization of a saint, the *Actes* function to confer the final stamp of authenticity on the materials from which the author has fashioned it; Foxe's powers of determination are supreme. The reader is required to accede to them.[7] The reader then acts on the suggestions in Foxe's work, researching in other texts indicated by Foxe the supplementary data that corroborate and substantiate the *Actes*.  The reader is put through an apprenticeship by Foxe, wherein she learns to enter into narrative, to participate in the full textual field of multiple genres that Foxe deploys.  Warren Wooden reads Foxe in a literary sense, noting that the *Actes* is not a univalent theological work, but rather includes many literary genres. "As an anatomy, Foxe's book includes a medley of literary forms, in prose and verse, ranging from sermons, tracts and epistles to doggerel rimes."[8] Such mixture of genres is also characteristic of de Bèze, who incorporates portions of his own poetry into *Icones,* as well as d'Aubigné, who refers to and at times cites from other of his more explicitly literary works in *Les tragiques*.  The inclusion of explicitly literary forms in what appears to be a theological or historical compilation would seem to substantiate the validity of a literary reading of the martyrologies.

## Telling the Story

Foxe tends much more toward narrative summary and dramatic presentation than toward Crespin's strategy of compilation and citation with (what may seem) minimal authorial intervention.  He differs from d'Aubigné's strategy of judicious selection and lapidary construction "pour esmouvoir," and he does not emphasize the tensions between word and image, word and body that so obsess de Bèze.  Rather, his theme might be summarized as that of readership.  In the *Actes,* he enacts the fullest dialogue of reader with book.  The book is always written, and rendered dynamic, in that region between Foxe and reader: a relationship of voice and response arises wherein the reader's right reaction is nearly as crucial as Foxe's statement.  "But this very complaint doth only touch them, who professing a perfectness of spiritual life above all the rest of the common sort of the people and who ought to be the masters of pity and godliness, yet shall you scarcely find any men more venomous in hatred, anger, malice, avenging, and all kinds of tyranny."  (99) The reader is asked to validate Foxe's constation through his own investigation which devolves from his experience of reading the book.  The zone into which the reader enters is always, primarily, that of story-telling. "We will begin the *narration* of this our *history* with the *story* and *tractation...*" (791; my emphasis). Despite the exhaustive historical documentation of the *Actes,* what Foxe sees as fundamentally characteristic of his work is its emphasis on an effective story: "It would fill another volume to comprehend the acts ... of all those who in other countries, at the rising of the gospel, suffered for the same. But praised be the Lord, every region almost hath its own history-writer, who sufficiently hath discharged that part of duty, as every one in matters of his own country is best acquainted: wherefore I shall the less need to overstrain my travail, or to overcharge this volume therewith; only it shall suffice me to collect three or four histories ... to bring into ... a story." (VI, 365). Through reading many stories, the reader comes to know doctrinal truth as Foxe believes it.

The ability to speak is therefore fundamental in Foxe's depiction of the martyrs. They are frequently presented as possessing miraculous powers to confound and silence their tormentors. (This is in contrast to the inflection of the documentation offered in the *Histoire des martyrs,* wherein the martyrs' primary trait is their willingness to *add* words to the words of their persecutors, their desire to write more and to confess more rather than to silence their persecutors). Speech is necessary so that a story may be created and recounted. The martyrs experience textual Pentecosts, in which the Word of the Spirit comes to reinforce their human word. This phenomenon echoes the strategy of Foxe's self-associa-tion with Christ. The story that evolves is thus always voiced by the martyr's strong word rather than through the interrogation constructed by Catholics (whereas in Crespin, the martyr's word defines itself against the Catholic questioning which impels it): in Foxe, while court proceedings are meticulously recorded, their stenography is ultimately preempted by the martyr, who silences the Catholics' questions. "But these are fierce brags and stout promises, with the subtle practices of these bishops, who thought themselves so sure before, the Lord against whom no determina-tion of man's counsel can prevail, by a small occasion did easily confound and overthrow. For the day of the examination being come, a certain personage the prince's court, and yet of no noble birth, named Lewis Clifford entering in among the bishops commanded them that they should not proceed with any definitive sentence against John Wickliff. At these words they were all amazed, and their combs so cut, that they became mute and speechless, as men having not one word in their mouths to answer." (V, 23).

The martyr's word is portrayed as succinct and efficacious. It is contrasted with the image of the confusion that prevailed at the tower of Babel, for the words of the persecutors are deemed senseless and ineffective. "Here is not to be passed over the great miracle of God's divine admonition and warning; for when the archbishop and suffragans, with the other doctors of divinity and lawyers, with a great company of *babbling* friars and religious persons, were gathered together to consult as touching John Wickliff, books, and that whole sect; when as I say, they were gathered together ... the very hour and instant that they should go forth with their business, a wonderful and terrible earthquake fell throughout all England ... whereby [they] thought it good to leave off from their determinate purpose" (V, 23).

The martyr always does have the last word in Foxe's text. To demonstrate this, it is customary for Fox, after his collection of documentation concerning sentencing and martyrdom, to append the martyr's letters. That is, *after* the martyr's body has been destroyed, the body of the text recuperates his speech, or epistolary body, and again speaks that word the Catholics had thought to silence. Such a documentary appendix also inscribes, for the perceptive reader, the method the reader herself should follow in reconstituting the textual body of the martyr. The emphasis is not on reading the dispersal of the body, but on the recuperation of the word. Crespin, de Bèze, d'Aubigné and Foxe all concur in this regard. Foxe does record a process of oscillation between body and word in his text; the emphasis moves back and forth between the two, leaving the reader to determine which is the most significant. We see this varying focus on body or on word in the account of Hierosme of Prague's trial: "And herein he showed himself marvellous *eloquent*; yea, never more. And when his oration was interrupted many times by divers of them carping at his sentences as he was speaking, yet there was none of all those that interrupted him who escaped unblancked; but he brought them all to confusion and *put them to silence* ... then was he again carried into prison, and was *grievously fettered* by the hands, arms and feet, with great chains and fetters of iron." (522)

While Foxe usually records the process of martyrdom in extraordinary detail, he does not always transcribe all of the martyr's speech (because he is unable to find adequate documents or, more frequently, because he feels himself surpassed by the task). Thus, we *see* vivid images of the death and dispersal of the body: "When all the wood was burned and consumed, the upper part of the body was left hanging in the chain, which they threw down stake and all, and making a new fire, burned it, the head being first cut into small gobbets ... the heart, which was found among the bowels, being well-beaten with stakes and clubs, was at last pricked upon a small stick, and roasted at a fire apart until it was consumed. Then, with great diligence gathering the ashes together, they cast them into the river." (494) We visualize in elaborate physiological images what happened to the body of the martyr. An "unvigilant" reader might perceive only the body and not realize the significance of the martyr's speech, however. To obviate this oversight, Foxe continually professes his inadequacy to fully render the power of the word, thereby alerting the reader to its importance: "No one can sufficiently write, or note, those things which he most eloquently, profoundly and philosophically had spoken in the said audience, neither can any tongue sufficiently declare the same; wherefore I have but only touched here the superficial matter of his talk, partly and not wholly, noting the same." (523) Occasionally, Foxe is able to use the image of the body to magnify the martyr's speech, as when Jerome is burned: "he moved continually his mouth and lips, as though he had still prayed or spoken within." (525)

## Compensatory Images and the Intercessory Text

Nevertheless, Foxe's reliance on images — while tempered by his constant reference to the word — is one factor which marks him as a transitional figure between hagiography and martyrology. Warren Wooden makes the case that Foxe added images to his text in order to strengthen it, to add a visual dimension to it. This was perhaps a strategy to reach those readers who might not measure up to the ideal of vigilance he had postulated. After having composed a work in which he was at times required to engage in compensatory tactics in order to be sure that the reference to the body would not overwhelm the presence of the word, Foxe later seemed to feel that such compensation was not in itself sufficient. By the time of the second printing he had devised the strategy of attempting to portray the emotive effect of the martyrdoms through imagery. Such imagery obviously could not portray the word; only a text that recorded the word to be read could do that. If only the word of the martyr was significant, Foxe could have let the *Actes* stand without images, for all that was essential was already contained in it, to be read by those who were able. Yet, aware that less competent readers might thereby be barred knowledge of the crucial confession contained in the *Actes*, Foxe gave his book an intercessory status. Rather than challenge the reader to read the written word alone, it would facilitate at least partial comprehension through the incorporation of imagery. Wooden comments on the *Actes'* "technical presentation ... physically imposing and appealing as an artifact. From the engraved title page ... to the more than 160 illustrations in the editions of the 1570s and later, the pictures contained a potent argument accessible even to the illiterate ... Foxe often coordinated his text with the engravings he had commissioned, calling the reader's attention to specific illustrations."[10] While the other Calvinist martyrologists, particularly Crespin and d'Aubigné, associate the image with the Catholic adoration of enclosed presence, and while de Bèze incorporates imagery in *Icones* only to surpass it and privilege the word, the Anglican Foxe tailors his text to point to, and thereby implicitly confer value on, the image.[11]

Foxe's use of the image to create accessibility of the text to the reader parallels his use of himself in the text. He constantly comments on his text, using his own textual body as an indicator to his reader of what he finds to be especially significant. His presence in the text, represented not only by the references to himself but also by the corpus of marginal commentary that skirts the body of the text, acts like the stylized figures of the pointing hand used in the typography of the *Histoire des martyrs*. It guides and influences the pattern of reading. In this way, Foxe creates a dynamic tension between impartial historical fact and the overlay of interpretation. The factual base suggests to the Protestant reader that he is receiving an accurate record of historical fact rather than an amalgam of legendary materials such as filled the Catholic saints' lives.[12] Indeed, all the Protestant martyrologies are characterized by the juxtaposition of history with the author's own narrative of history. A phenomenon of textual layering uses history as the foundation, but converts it from neutral fact into subjectively-inflected speech. The intense personalization of the Protestant accounts is their trademark, while hagiographies are typified by anonymity. The Protestant martyrologies are more similar to the category established by Père Delahaye of "passions épiques," a term he uses "pour désigner des récits de martyre où l'hagiographe en use envers l'histoire de son héros avec l'extrême liberté qu'ont de tout temps revendiqué les poètes."[13] However, the Protestant narratives do not create a fictional or legendary account as do the hagiographers.[14] Instead, they create a personal account, in which they themselves enter a factual base as a literary inscription. The reader has to deal with the author as visible and audible actor in the work. Foxe obsessively addresses the reader, reminding him of his presence. Foxe self-consciously writes to be read; he constantly refers to the reader's reception of his endeavor: "Hitherto thou hast *heard*, Christian reader! the lamentable persecutions of these latter days ... In the *reading* thereof ... the knowledge and *reading* whereof shall not be lost to Christians." (V, 79) He here equates reading with hearing, word with speech, translating his intent to make the *Actes* an effective text. The exclamation point underlines the verbal quality of the statement.

The address to the reader, from a personalized, determinate authorial persona, is typical of the Protestant accounts, and does not occur in the hagiographies. Foxe's reference to himself is not abstract, nor is his figuring of the reader within his text. He uses explicitly bodily metaphors, describing in detailed anatomy his own position, that of his opponents, and that of the reader. His enumeration of body parts is reminiscent of the roll call of the martyrs' severed limbs. He addresses the Catholics as though they were physically present: "How will you be able to *stand* in his sight when he shall appear? With what *face* shall ye look upon the Lord, whose servants ye have slain? Or with what *hearts* will you be able to behold the bright *face* of them whom you set so proudly here condemning..." (xiii; my emphasis). Here, the dissection of the Catholic body reverses the dismemberment the Catholics had effected of Protestant bodies. The text acts like an instrument of torture on the would-be torturers, negating on their bodies the effect of their actions. Foxe also describes his own role in the text. He shows that it is his task to textually reassemble the fragments of the martyrs' bodies. In the following account, he uses a story of a miraculous occurrence to figure his own actions. "...A prodigious narration ... of a brute ox, which, being in the fields and seeing the carcasses of the dead bodies [of martyrs] so cut in two, made a loud noise ... and afterwards, coming to the quarters of one of the dead bodies lying in the field, first took up the one half, and then coming again, took up likewise the other half, and so, as he could, joined them both together, which being espied by those who saw the doing of the brute ox, and marvelling thereat ... he commanded the quarters again to be brought where they were before, to prove whether the beast would [join them again] ; who faileth not (as the author recordeth) but, in like sort as before, taking up the fragments of the dead corpse laid them again together.    It followeth more in the author ... " (820) The intercalation of the mention of the author into this anecdote stresses the similar function. The symbolic role of the account in figuring the author's role is thereby signalled.

Thus, the use of bodily imagery is significant in the *Actes*. Foxe's reliance on imagery situates him at a transitional point between Catholics and Calvinists, in that he does not hesitate to incorporate imagery. However, his treatment of this imagery is closer to that of the Calvinists, and de Bèze in particular, because of the statements he makes condemning reliance on imagery at the same time that he includes it in his text.[15] Such comments as those which follow create a problem in Foxe's text, for they point to the unreliability of the image: "Johannes Ramus ... maketh mention of the image of the crucifix being there ... which the Turk took, and writing this superscription upon the head of it, 'Hic est christianorum Deus,' ... gave it to his soldiers to be scorned and ... made every man to spit at it most contumeliously. Wherein thou hast, good reader, by the way to note, what occasion of slander and offence we Christians give unto the barbarious infidels by this our ungodly superstition, in having images in our temples, contrary to the express commandment of God in his word. For if St. Paul writing to the Corinthians sayeth, 'We know Christ no more after the flesh,' how much less then is Christ to be known of us in blind stocks and images set up in our temples ... Images and plain idolatry ..." (IV, 31-39).

We note the Catholic attempt to turn symbol into actual body; the "head" of the cross, rather than a neutral term such as the "top," indicates the human form. In this quotation, Foxe moves from image to word (the citation of St. Paul), back to images again, figuring the oscillation in his text between the two. It is as though Foxe would prefer to eliminate imagery, but fears an inability to fully communicate without it. His attempt seems to be to legitimize textual images through a strategy of reversal: if the image is that which is present only to be surpassed by the word, then image is not threatening, for it itself testifies to the power of the word. Like the mother in the following anecdote, Foxe seeks to reconfigure the image, to conform it to the word. "John Clerc ... for which his punishment was this, that three several days he should be whipped, and afterwards have a mark imprinted on his forehead, as a note of infamy. His mother, being a Christian woman ... when she beheld her son thus ... deformed in the face, constantly and boldly did encourage her son, crying with a loud voice, 'Blessed be Christ! and welcome be *his* prints and marks! '" (IV, 361; my emphasis)

We note that the deformation is only facial; the Catholics do not penetrate to the essence of the man, but only make their nefarious mark superficially. The mother renames the mark as Christ's stamp, thereby converting the destructive intent of the image into victorious speech. The pains of the body will be palliated and exalted by the invocation of the word: the body is therefore paradoxically necessary so that the word may reign supreme. This is a metaphoric reversal of the bodying forth of Christ, in which the Word is at the origin, and then is made flesh. The *Actes* even contains instances in which the torments of the body are effectively canceled out by the word. Although Foxe usually dwells in great detail on the torture of the martyr, on occasion he omits such details, as though to demonstrate that the word is his essential focus. In his recounting of the martyrdom of George Carpenter, no account is provided of his torture. The spoken name of Christ dominates throughout. "He answered: 'This shall be my sign and token, that so long as I can open my mouth, I will not cease to call upon the name of Jesus.' Behold, good reader! what an incredible constancy was in this godly man, such as lightly hath not been seen in any way before. His face and countenance changed colour, but cheerfully he went into the fire ... When he was laid upon the ladder, and the hangman put a bag of gunpowder about his neck, he said, 'Let it be so, in the name of the Father and of the Son and of the Holy Ghost ...' In a loud voice he cried out, 'Jesus! Jesus!' Then the hangman turned him over, and he again for a certain space cried, 'Jesus! Jesus!' and so yielded up his spirit." (VI, 376) The bodily alterations are insignificant when compared with the ability to confess the Word (although nonetheless the body is necessary to physically speak it). As in the story of the young man who was branded, George Carpenter takes a punishment and redefines it as God's will. He respeaks in his own sense, and Foxe rewrites, the Catholic attempt to mutilate his body, as an exaltation of his spirit. Outward seeming is misleading; it is inner coherence which conveys truth. Foxe thus reverses what he finds to have transpired in Catholic religious observance: "thou mayest understand, gentle reader, how the religion of Christ which consisted only in spirit and verity, was wholly turned into outward observations, ceremony and idolatry. So many saints we had, so many gods ... so many relics forged and feigned ... How the people were led ... instead of God's word, man's word was set up." (VI, 250) Foxe calls for a particular, discerning reader who will be able to distinguish appearance from reality, and he opposes this new sort of reading to what he deems Catholic misreading: "But the cardinal would hear no scriptures; he disputed without scriptures; he devised glosses and expositions out of his own head, and by distinctions ... like a very proteus he avoided all things." (IV, 271). Here, it is revealing that, just as in the account of the degradation of the crucifix by the Turks, a bodily part is mentioned, although construed figuratively, in reference to the cardinal: his head, a metonym for the rest of his body, locates untruth in the Catholic body. By opposition, truth is therefore to be found in the body of the Protestant martyr. The body of the martyrs is therefore necessarily wholly unlike that of the Catholic. Indeed, the textual body inscribed in the *Actes* (and other Protestant martyrologies) is a changed and reconfigured shape. Even Foxe's manner of gathering documentation about the body entails a joining of pieces in an odd, seemingly haphazard way, as though the exact fit of bone to ligament to bone were not significant. For instance, Foxe recites the death of Thomas Moutard, martyr. Then he editorializes, "This Dutch story should have gone before with the Dutch martyrs [were he constructing an account dependent on mirroring organic order] but seeing Valenciennes is not distant from France, it is not much out of order to adjoin the same with the French martyrs; who, at length, shall be joined together in the kingdom of Christ." (VII, 446). Here, it is clear that Christ will resurrect the physical body; it is Foxe's task to compose its textual phantom.

### Corporeal Conduits

Textual resurrection does not aim at constructing an anatomically- correct physiology of the martyr. What is significant is the use of reference to the body as a path to the word. The hodgepodge of physical pieces does not create the likeness of the physical body, but rather provokes a sort of sustained auditory hallucination requiring attention to the martyr's word. In like fashion, many of the descriptions of martyrdoms effectively turn the martyr's body into a text through its close association (and condemnation) with its personal, textual production. Dr. Basssinet is martyred, sandwiched literally and figuratively between his books: "the judges ... where he was examined in this form as followeth: 'Hast thou not set forth to sale [sic] the Bible and the New Testament in French? The prisoner answered that he had so done ... Hereupon he was immediately condemned to be burned, and ... for a sign or token of the same cause of his condemnation, he carried *two Bibles hanging about his neck, the one before and the other behind him*: but this poor man had also the word of God in his heart and in his mouth and ceased not continually by the way until he came to the place of execution to exhort and admonish the people to read the holy Scriptures." (VII, 487). Thus, even his final words are not his individual speech, but rather the words of the Book.[16] The location of the body, so crucial for hagiographies in providing a site for the worship of the saint, is used in Foxe also to point to a textual phenomenon: the body becomes a place-marker for the reading of the Word: "This John Randall being a young scholar in Christ's college ... for the love of the Scripture and sincere religion, he began not only to be suspect but also hated ... his study door being broken open ... the young man was found [hanged] in such sort and manner that he had his face looking upon the Bible, and his finger pointing to a place of Scripture, wherein predestination was treated of." (VIII, 694) The viewer of this macabre scene is compelled to become a reader. He is urgently drawn beyond the sight of the corpse to read for himself the message the stiffened finger designates. While yet using it as a vehicle, word surpasses body. And the book here is figured as a mediating entity between the body and the Word that he once read and that the reader now reads, symbolizing the purpose of the *Actes*.[17]

# Notes

1. Warren Wooden, *John Foxe* (Boston: Twayne, 1983), 30. "When ... attacked ... for naming as martyrs people like John Wycliffe, who died peacefully in his own bed, Foxe replied that such were 'faithful witnesses of Christ's truth and testament,' and, noting the word in Greek means 'witness bearer'..."

2. *Ibid.*, iii.

3. *Ibid.*, 42-54.

4. Joan Webber, *The Eloquent 'I'* (Madison, Wisconsin: University of Wisconsin Press, 1968), 51.

5. Wooden, 44.

6. Webber, 4.

7. It is true that Foxe did receive such information from readers. But unlike Crespin he never actively requested it.

8. Wooden, 42.

9. In his emphasis on narrative and on the content of the martyr's experience, Foxe and Crespin are more similar than de Bèze and d'Aubigné to the hagiographic genre. Cazelles specifies that "de fait, la matière, c'est-à-dire, l'élément narratif, prime sur le sens et la structure ... la source sert de preuve officielle, et ce qui est dit—la matière—compte plus que la manière de le dire." Brigitte de Cazelles, *Le corps de sainteté,* (Geneva: Droz, 1982), 186. Foxe and Crespin differentiate their accounts, however, by the framing techniques they employ to indicate their authorial supervision and manipulation of the material they collect. In hagiographies, "le cadre explicatif (prologue et épilogue) est singulièrement moins imaginatif et moins développé que la séquence médiane." Cazelles, 186. In Crespin and Foxe, however, this textual apparatus of presentation is of the utmost importance.

10. Wooden, 49.

11. Foxe and de Bèze are similar in their use of images in at least one respect, however. Warren Wooden notes that in the *Actes* "the small conventional engravings of the martyrs which are scattered throughout the text ... the same engravings are used repeatedly for different martyrs without any pretense of

being original portraits for individual martyrs (although the names are changed for each)", 49.

12. Wooden, 58.

13. René Aigrain, *L'hagiographie: ses sources, sa méthode, son histoire* (Paris: Bloud et Gay, 1953), summarizing le Père Delehaye, 140.

14. Aigrain, 131. "Qu'il y ait dans les 'légendes hagiographiques' telles que nous les définissons en commençant, des 'légendes' au sens péjoratif, qu'elles se mêlent à l'histoire dans la trame de certains récits ... il ne nous est pas possible d'en douter." De Certeau explicitly employs the term 'fiction' in discussing these texts: "l'extraordinaire et le possible s'appuient l'un l'autre pour construire la fiction ici mise en service de l'exemplaire." de Certeau, *L'Ecriture de l'histoire*, 279.

15. Foxe, *The Actes and Monuments of the Martyrs* (New York: AMS Press, 1964), IV, 20. "Therefore, saying my judgement in this behalf ... This hope I have, and do believe, that when the church of Christ alone shall be received to be our justifier, all other religions, merits, traditions, images, patrons and advocates set apart." All other references to Foxe are to this text.

16. Here is where the usefulness of Foucault's paradigm of the disciplined body and the "genre of the condemned man's final speech" breaks down, because the final speeches Foucault describes (1) either validate social order by respeaking the need for the punitive inscription—that is, the victim has been effectively socially-coerced, or (2) create a rebellious, individual speech that refuses to confirm the societal indictment. In the case of the Protestant martyr, neither of the above ordinarily apply (although the second may be discerned, secondarily, in the *author*). Rather, the martyr gives himself up; he respeaks the word of another: God.

17. This is in direct contrast to the ultimate effect of the hagiography, in which the focus remains squarely on the body. Indeed, Delehaye notes that "il est pour le moins étrange que la parole de l'Evangile, qui aurait, à ce qu'on suppose, guidé la plume des hagiographes, ne soit jamais citée par eux, ou qu'ils n'y fassent aucune allusion." Père Hippolyte Delehaye, *Les passions des martyrs et les genres littéraires* (Brussels, 1921), 112.

# Reconstituting the Textual Body in Jean Crespin's *Histoire des martyrs* (1564)

Jean Crespin, a Reformed editor in Geneva, was a contemporary of Théodore de Bèze. His major contribution to the history of the Reformation is a stunningly compendious project, several volumes of a *Histoire des martyrs* which spans decades in the contemporary history of Protestant persecution, reaching back as well into the early Christian church. Studded with first-hand testimony and eyewitness documentation, it is a massive enterprise testifying to Crespin's desire to uphold the Calvinist faith and to display the Genevan church as the true church. The *Histoire des martyrs* also makes valuable connections with other Protestant movements, recounting martyrdoms and reproducing confessional statements from England, Germany, the Netherlands, Scotland and elsewhere.

While at first the compilation appears exhaustively encyclopedic, further examination reveals another characteristic: that of personal, authorial intervention, rather than manipulation by a merely editorial personality. Crespin employs a strategy of inscription which superimposes texts and bodies. The aim is ultimately to convert body into text, text which will mirror divine Word: the transmutation of flesh into *Logos*. It is this attempt which licenses a literary investigation and not simply a theological or historical interpretation of the work. Crespin's ceaseless sensitivity to the projected response of his reader creates an interactive textual theater.

Jean Crespin's *Histoire des martyrs* (written 1554-1597) appears at first as a collection of fragments supplying historical information regarding the martyrdoms of continental Protestant men and women. However, I argue that this martyrology is far more sophisticated and coherent in its conception and execution than its episodic appearance conveys in a first reading.[1] It aims not merely at a tendentious recounting of persecution. Rather, the text seeks to effect a veritable resuscitation of the bodies upon which it is structured, those suffocated words still contained in the stricken corpse. It initially seems that no authorial manipulation of the materials occurs. Crespin appears to act in the role of editor of the data he has gathered together.[2]   Yet I hope to show that he has carefully composed this assemblage with the intention of conveying his  conception of Christian martyrdom to the reader.  And this particular formulation is predicated on the collected corpus of testimonies becoming the *corps,* the corpse, of the dead who live again through their word.

In his short study of several Protestant martyrologies, Leon Halkin asserts that "la parenté entre les divers Martyrologies s'explique ... par une similitude des préoccupations chez leurs auteurs".[3] He does not note that Crespin's *Histoire* is unique; it is the great ancestor of the other Protestant martyrologies. Halkin characterizes Protestant martyrs in this way:  "les protestants évitent toute vénération attribuant à la personne du martyr un véritable pouvoir d'intercession.  Il n'en est pas moins vrai qu'ils décrivent les gestes de leurs héros avec le même désir émerveillé qui se retrouve dans toutes les hagiographies"[4]. Crespin stands out because he does not manifest the "lyrisme" that Halkin finds characteristic of both hagiographical and martyrological writing. First, Crespin usually does not narrate, but rather allows the documents he has compiled to speak for themselves.  Secondly, when he does narrate, despite the amassing of painful details, his voice is terse in the extreme.  He consciously effaces his own verbal presence in order to allow the physical absence of the martyrs to be mediated by their new, verbal presence generated by their inclusion in the book.  Finally, and perhaps most significantly, Halkin's point that intercession is denied to the person is well-taken, for Crespin intends that the book be itself the locus of salvific potential.

### Fragments and Bodies

Crespin's methodology in creating a site of textual resurrection emphasizes the manner of the arrangement[5] of the materials of the compendium.  The result is a textual body, rather than disparate fragments.  What is included, where it is located, how frequently portions repeat or are echoed, the refrains of the martyrs' speeches and letters compose a litany of which, despite the length of the material, portions cry out to be read aloud. Crespin also asserts the fundamental corporality of the martyrs' language: their words imitate, mime, rehearse (and ultimately surpass and negate) their suffering. The *Histoire des martyrs* cannot be read as history alone, or as a recuperative epistolary endeavor; it must be read as stories of bodies, bodies that become speech, speech that exalts word and Word.

The book itself is composed of parts, just as a body has members. Similarly, these parts interrelate and conjoin to achieve textual organicity. The *Histoire des martyrs* is composed of twelve books, the last two of which are appendices added at a later date. The books are preceded by a lengthy corpus of prefatory material: an "Epistre à l'église"; a letter "Aux persécuteurs de l'église"; a poem "aux persécuteurs de l'église de Jésus Christ"; and an emblematic poem dedicated to "la constance des martyrs fidèles de nostre seigneur Jésus Christ". Particularly significant in this group is the incorporation of image into word; most Protestant emblem books are written later than this date[6] and as the chapter on de Bèze will attempt to show, a certain problematic as to the appropriate use of imagery and pictorial representation arises for the theologically iconoclastic Calvinists.[7] Here, the inclusion of the emblem as a liminary piece, *en tête*, to use a bodily image, of the work, may suggest that something physical, visible in the text, here will be included. Word and image (the martyr's confession plus the portrayal of the suffering body) conjoin in the *Histoire des martyrs* in an emblematic way, fleshing each other out, complementing and deepening each other's meaning. Finally, a substantial preface relates the martyrs upon whom Crespin proposes to scaffold his work to those martyrs of the early Christian church. Throughout, it is clear that this is a polemical work aimed at upholding the Protestant church, the "body" of the faithful. Crespin expresses three aims. He suggests a didactic account for the edification of the faithful, a collection of testimonies for the confirmation of faith, and indicates that he is here supplying the material for a sort of supplementary church history: "Je vous y présente; en somme, la matière d'une belle histoire Ecclésiastique, qui montre la même façon de laquelle Dieu l'a de tout temps conduite et gouvernée" (ii). Crespin in this assertion disavows authorial involvement[8], designating his text as the raw material from which someone might later extract elements for incorporation into a coherent history. We shall find, however, that Crespin crafts these materials in such a way as to shape our narrative understanding of them.[9] His desire to be humbly self-effacing as an author is counteracted by the strong sense of divine inspiration he feels. Like many other Protestant writers[10], and like the writers of the Gospels (who also, it could be argued, seek to reconstitute Christ's body through fragments of his teaching) Crespin believes that he acts here to transmit the divine Word[11]. It would seem therefore that these materials should require little reworking, since they are creations of God. Perhaps for this reason, many of the martyrs' statements are recorded verbatim, with no alteration. Crespin does, however, frame these texts with his own words and beliefs, thus modifying their statement and inflecting their reception. He also juxtaposes them with similar texts, creating a dialogue effect among the sources[12]. Patterns of proximity create the impression of a multitude of proselytizing speakers.

The *Histoire* includes several different sorts of documentation. Records of trials or inquisitorial proceedings, letters written by other Protestants to the martyr, and eyewitness accounts of martyrdoms stud the text with varying kinds of testimonies. Most interesting, however, are those occasions on which Crespin himself narrates the event of a martyrdom. He always labels these accounts "histoires"[13] and it would seem that he means that term to be taken at its full French face value: these narrations are both "history" and "story." His accounts are characterized by a great deal of detail, an emphasis on spectacle which is lacking in the other sources, and the use of didactic emphasis. Most markedly, it would seem that the emphasis on bodily parts before, during and after torture, and the concern for the dismembered and the potentially rehabilitatible body, are present in the documents that Crespin includes, as well as being a particular focus of his own.

The narratives that Crespin himself constructs provide clues as to the manner of reading the compendium. Most obvious in this regard is a small tract entitled "Traité des afflictions et persécutions qui aviennent ordinairement aux fidèles." This tract, of Crespin's own composition, concludes Book One of the *Histoire,* and seems designed to function as yet another liminary piece. The large number of prefatory remarks would seem to substantiate the likelihood that Crespin feels a need to indicate to the reader how the *Histoire* should be received. The "Traité", which we shall examine shortly, suggests certain themes to which the reader should attend while perusing the *Histoire*. Indeed, there exists within the *Histoire* a paradigm for reading, elaborated within the interstices linking one piece of documentation to another. The amount of occasions on which the actual words of the martyrs are recorded, juxtaposed with their own earlier or later writings, apposed to that which contemporaries have to say about them, creates a multi-layered text that is analogous, in its operation, to an act of reassemblage. The dissassembled martyr, torn and tortured at his death, is piece by piece reassembled textually, as Crespin creates a cut-and-piece mosaic of the martyr's words and actions. This layering, it should be noted, operates differently from the phenomenon experienced by Catholic saints, for instance. Catholic saints were customarily cut into pieces, so that various fragments could be distributed to churches and holy sites. The fragments of the body were believed to contain immanent efficacy. The dispersal of the body in this way amounted to a form of triumph over space: the dismembered body dominated more extensively by the very act of disunion which annihilated its original organic wholeness. Here, because Protestants did not acknowledge or venerate enclosed presence, it was impossible that portions of the Protestant martyrs' bodies function in the sense of relics. Therefore, reassemblage of the body—as a speaking self—was required. Since the Catholics took great care to eradicate all traces of the heretic body, breaking and pulverizing bones, consuming the body in fire so that only ashes remained, the only possibility for such an act of reconstitution was literary. The collected words and enunciations of the martyr stood symbolically for those parts of the body which had been destroyed. An effective arrangement of these portions could construct the articulated skeleton of the martyr's testimonial speech. In this manner, Crespin's text defies death, battles the superimposition of Catholic upon Protestant discourse, and, in the *Histoire's* assertion that, through inclusion in this text, the martyr cannot die[14], through narrative resuscitates the martyr. While explicitly and repeatedly denigrating Catholic reliquaries, this text is nevertheless in some sense like a reliquary, in that it carefully houses the precious remnants of the martyr's existence, his speech and last acts.[15] Unlike a reliquary, however, it does not provide a spatial, localized place, but rather, through its emphasis on orality and textuality, works to disperse enclosed presence: it is a textual presence, which is to say, nowhere and everywhere; the word, infinitely disseminated, speaks in, through and beyond all physical bounds. The intermingling of images of corporality and discourse strengthens the interdependence of body and word—the lost body as the point of departure for the impetus to valorize the word to recuperate a new, textual body.[16] For example, the martyrs often voluntarily choose to substitute their own blood for ink when the prisonkeeper refuses to provide a sufficient supply of the writing implement. Crespin's safekeeping of a document that is literally constituted in, and through, a part of the martyr's physical body is, at least in appearance, like to the conservation of a relic, a severed finger or head or bone, but in intention such preservation works quite differently in the *Histoire des martyrs*: the paper inscribed with blood constitutes a tool in the project to body forth, textually, the word that once inhabited the now lost body. In addition, the image of the martyr that is finally constituted is very clearly an anti-relic, an anti-idol. Crespin enjoins, "ne vous amusons point à faire réserve de leurs cendres ou de leurs ossements; ce sont choses mortes, mais revoyans les vivans en leurs responses, lettres et disputes, et mémoires de leur constance." (2) Very clearly, the body is not resurrected in a corporeally recognizable form (just as the resurrected body of Christ was "changed"[17]), but rather the body undergirds, and is displayed in, the speech uttered while the body was yet extant. Crespin always takes care that references to images be subordinated to speech: images for him are uniquely constituted through speech (there are no woodcuts associated with the text, unlike de Bèze's *Icones*). Also, images are usually associated in the *Histoire* with superstition and idolatry (crosses, figures of saints, *sambénits* or inquisition hats upon which symbols of damnation have been painted). When enough portions of physically-inscribed documents conjoin in the *Histoire*, the martyr appears in a reintegrated, physical form, "conforme" to Christ. The martyr's conformity is identifiable, yet changed in that through the process of martyrdom, he has become "conforme" to Christ: the flesh has become Word, a material which enfleshes the text in a cycle of narrative renewal. Crespin speaks of the *Histoire* as being a sort of portrait gallery ("comme en tableaux naïfs") wherein one may view inspirational exempla, but he never lets it be forgotten that the viewer is always intended to interact with the representation: "en somme, qui voudrait contempler la condition et l'estat des fidèles de l'Eglise chrestienne en ces derniers temps, pourrait comme en tableaux naïfs, ces livres le nous figurent par vives couleurs, voire et en particulier présentent un chacun comme en miroirs luisans, comment on se doit porter ... pour les représenter devant les yeux." (34) These exempla themselves possess efficacy.

In a second paradigm of reading in the *Histoire,* martyrs write letters detailing their suffering to the faithful. These destinators retain the letters, or copies of them, which they later convey to Crespin. Roland Bainton, examining John Foxe's *Acts of the Martyrs,* is "amazed at the measure of communication between those in and out of prison ... chiefly by way of correspondence."[18] Scripture speaks of the disciples as bodily epistles[19]. In their prolific epistolary activity, the martyrs deliberately define themselves in faith as other than that which "law" has made them. In so doing, they abstract their body from physical confinement, and disseminate their word throughout space. Their body, even prior to their death, begins to become word, a word that speaks the Word, the Word which resuscitates the body of Christ. Crespin displays these letters, for which we then become new, secondary destinators, and toward which we experience a reaction. It is hoped by both Crespin, and to a certain, unintentional, general degree, by the martyr, that our reaction will produce an affective chiasmus; it will return us to the beginning, and mirror the emotions that the martyr experienced. If this response is produced, that in turn validates the project of the *Histoire* (and of the martyr's life). That is why Crespin calls for a certain kind of reader, and a proper disposition in one's reading, to secure the success of his project. He invites" à ce sacré travail ceux qui peuvent y servir" (725), a "Lecteur fidèle" (724), someone who, by the intensity of meditation on Crespin's collection, will reactivate the martyrs' words, for, he warns, "qui se vient en ce lieu adresser/Pour voir, ouyr, et non pour penser,/ Voyant, oyant, il ne voit, et n'oit goute" (11). The reader's meditation on the book's *matière* (a term possessing in Randle Cotgrave's dictionary of 1611 the sense both of matter from which text is formed and bodily substance) gives it the impetus required to transform it from a text, into a reconstituted body. The musing on the martyrs' words inevitably refers back to the broken body, source of the confession of faith. This pattern can potentially continue infinitely, for the *Histoire* is an expandable book, one to which readers are continually invited to contribute: "cependant nous désirons et prions tous ceux qui en savent quelque chose (comme il seroit impossible à un homme seul de recueillir ce que mil cent meurtriers ont perpétué), à mettre en lumière ..." (706) The actual, human and limited book of the compiler is here overwhelmed by the bodies of all the dead he intends to memorialize; a third body is called to step into the breach, to participate, to lighten the load: the reader takes upon him- or herself the burden of that bodily surplus through reading.

Each contribution to the martyrology reactivates the referential quality of the narrative. The mirror metaphor is further reinforced by the fact that some martyrs communicate among themselves; in the case of the Cinq Escholiers à Lyon, the five write an extensive, mutually hortative correspondence, reflecting each to the other their concerns and sources of strength: "Ces cinq Escholiers de Jésus Christ, durant leur emprisonnement, non seulement se consoloyent mutuellement les uns les autres par missives, mais aussi les amis et les Eglises de Gèneve et Lausanne leur escrivoyent lettres" (225). The recipient often echoes the phrasing of the letter to which he responds, reflecting an inspirational discourse that is then communicated to the reader, for it is taken up again in the textual body of the *Histoire* through its unerring reiteration.

Above all, Crespin hopes that the words of the martyr will be revivified through their inclusion in his text: "Ce sont eux mesmes parlant en leurs écrits consolans et enseignans ceux qui restent encore en ceste course" (i). Unlike Théodore de Bèze and Agrippa d'Aubigné, who to different degrees and in different ways demonstrate authorial self-consciousness, Crespin nowhere explicitly emphasizes his own word: he states that his voice is an accessory of the martyrs: "et afin qu'on ne doute de la fidélité gardée en ces recueils, depuis que Dieu m'a fait la grâce d'en avoir jeté les premiers Commentaires, j'ai protesté et tasché d'escrire ce qui concerne spécialement l'estat des Eglises ... le plus succintement et simplement qu'il m'a esté possible, connoissant que vérité n'a besoin d'ornement ou parure en dehors d'elle." (3) Yet, to the extent that his accounts are in intimate proximity to those of the martyrs he includes (and in fact the two narratives are at times indistinguishable one from the other), he in this sense respeaks the martyrs' words and makes them his own. Also, to the degree that he attempts to direct the manner in which his text will be interpreted, he interposes his voice between the *Histoire* and the reader. In a palimpsest of bodies and texts (martyrs writing, martyrs reading, martyrs dying, martyrs' word recorded, martyrs' word read), Crespin enrolls himself in the list of martyrs. He experiences their tribulations vicariously and distills the lessons of faith and constancy to be learned from them, in his own words and fashion. Further, through the construction and composition of his compendium, Crespin lifts the events, people and places he describes out of their quotidian, worldly contingency, qualifying them according to a spiritual sense.[20] In this way, he focuses on a meta-reality, the divine purpose that informs and redeems the suffering here recorded.[21]

## (Em)bodying the Text

My methodology in approaching this text, and other Protestant martyrologies, is influenced by the school of textual materialist criticism[22] which seeks to recover substantiality in language.[23] The contention of this school, and of others not explicitly identified with it but equally interested in the relationship between body and language, is that "language is capable of registering in its own contours the weight of the material world ... that language itself may enter, act on and alter the material world."[24] The concerns of this school are similar to mine: the way in which a word may become enfleshed, the process through which violence done through speech is performed legibly on a body. In a description of martyrs of the early Church and of writings about them, Peter Brown notes that "it was upon the flesh of the martyrs and the *confessores* that the *saeculum* rained down its more terrible blows. There is a physicality in the writings of Cyprian that crackles with the same sense of the flesh as a charged boundary, under constant threat of violation. The 'glory' of martyrdom unfolds like dark red flowers in his pages ... to 'follow Christ' was nothing less than a daily martyrdom."[25] And in *Discipline and Punish,* Michel Foucault demonstrated the marks of the legal inscription of culpability upon the malefactor's body.

Crespin's *Histoire* is punctuated by such images of pain. Its pages are bloodstained with the martyrs' agonies, for their confessions, written in the blood of the martyrs, and the marks the persecutors make with their victims' blood, supply the matter of the book. In such a way Crespin's book acts as Elaine Scarry calls for language to act; the text should "lift the body into language ... [and] work to lift it out again ... relocated to the inside of some language-soaked artifact to whose form it now contributes."[26]   As the ashes of the martyrs' pulverized bones are dispersed by their destroyers, Crespin collects them in a textual columbarium. "Ils firent diligence de recueillir les cendres et les jettèrent dedans le Rhin, afin qu'ils ne restast rien de cest homme sur la terre, tant petit que ce fust. Toutesfois sa mémoire ne pourra jamais estre effacée du coeur des fidèles" (62). His text rehearses the fragments of their speech through the rearticulations of the pieces of their bodies. The ever-presence of the body (despite its dispersal, indeed absence) is apparent in the attention to the details of its destruction.

The incessant verbal onslaught of atrocities constitutes a physical block, a tortured corporality in and through textuality, that confronts the reader and demands acknowledgement. Even before the martyrdom, the body is a sort of text: "les afflictions sont les vrais commentaires de la Saincte Escriture" (vi); that is, the suffering body illumines the biblical pages, illustrating it, glossing it, commenting upon it in an intertextual relationship. The paper of the book is itself sentient: it has the capacity to experience and express suffering. "Le papier pleureroit si je récitais les blasphesmes horribles qui furent prononcez par ces monstres" (708). The *Histoire* both recalls the tortured, afflicted body of the martyr through the confessional utterance of the latter, and provokes the pain the reader experiences when confronted with its testimony. The text becomes a tissue (*textus*) like to sinews and skin, a system of words woven together to create a corporeal complex. Formulaic repetitions ("conforme," sceller de son sang," "nostre Seigneur Jésus Christ") constitute a textual mass which mimes the density of the speaking body.

It is a painful paradox that the *Histoire* could not have been written without the martyrdoms it contains. Two kinds of writing and two kinds of bodily experience form the poles of destruction and regeneration in the text. First, writing exacts the punishment of the martyr: the official legal decree is written, and rewritten as a symbol of degradation on the *sambénits* or on signs the martyrs are forced to wear. Paradoxically, while writing demands the execution of the body, this inscription also perishes with the body. "Il leva les yeux au ciel, et ployant le col, il fit tomber de sa teste ceste belle couronne de papier qu'on luy avoit mise. Lors l'un des satellites luy dit, Remettons la sur la teste afin qu'il soit bruslé ensemble avec ses maistres les Diables." (61)   Crespin then recuperates that writing which is organically linked to the defunct body: the statement the martyr wrote to declare Christian identity. These assembled written fragments respeak the words of the absent body, and resuscitate that corporeal source before the reader. Like a phoenix, the book rises from the martyrs' ashes, possessing a dual existence: itself as text, and itself as body (their broken bodies). Elaine Scarry describes how such a phenomenon transpires in language: "the verbal unit (word, sentence) is reconciled as a material unit, the page. But the whole page in turn must now be reconceived as capable, beyond its own material fragility, of somehow bearing this record of the material world ... [we experience] the substantiveness of language — its capacity to mime, and perhaps eventually acquire — the actual weight of what it describes."[27]

The martyrs' writings are stamped with the circumstances of their suffering: Crespin tears his pages back from the death that gave birth to them: "j'ay trouvé quelquesfois des choses obscures, comme escrites en cachots ténébreux, et souvent de sang que les pauvres Martyrs s'estoyent fait sortir, par faute d'encre" (3).   He confides that the model of the Cinq Escholiers à Lyon  motivates him to begin his compilation; just as they correspond, and preserve each other's letters and statements, so he is their successor in this archival activity, but only after their deaths is his role necessitated. He is an aweful intermediary between past pain and present perception of it, "servant d'un entredeux pour soutenir [leurs] discours" (38). He is a sort of posthumous correspondent, to the extent that he interacts with their discourse, and intends that the reader also interact with it. Crespin alludes to the creative paradox of martyrdom in the "Traité des afflictions", employing metaphors of containers cracked and vastated, so that their precious contents might be activated, just as incense serves no purpose until it is pulverized and set aflame: "... un grain de semence, qui ne montre jamais bien sa force que quand il a esté brisé dedans le mortier, ... la grape, qui ne monstre non plus la siene, jusques à ce qu'il a esté brisé dedans le mortier, ... l'encens et ... épices, qui ne rendent pas bien leur odeur, l'un qu'il ne soit mis et bruslé au feu, les autres qu'ils ne soyent menuisez et esmiez entre les doigts." (36)

One source for the text is that of the martyrs' confessions. The manner in which confessions function in the text recall the foregoing metaphors. The confessions are of two sorts: motivated confessions, the statement of the accused, obtained under duress; and unmotivated confessions, those outpourings of spiritual testimonial which the martyrs offer freely to the Lord. Most interesting is that, through the volition of the martyr[28] (as well as Crespin's editorializing,) the forced confessional compliance is reintegrated into the idiom of the martyr's voluntary witness. The martyrs are markedly eager to cooperate in their prosecution, to actually participate in the legal process: they want to have their say, and do so by appropriating the medium of the trial statement to their own purposes. That is, it is paradoxically because they are compelled to make a confession that they are able to fully formulate their expression of faith. The surrendering of their body to a hostile power enables their most free speech. They rush to place their signatures on their statements, offering to attest to their veracity in blood: "je veux signer ma confession première," cries Jeanne Ogvier, "et si ne la signe d'encre ce sera de mon sang" (388). Even the most unlettered of the martyrs (although most are very learned, citing Scripture copiously, and some are writers and printers) are aware that their bodies will become the parchment for two inscriptions: the first, destructive, a Catholic signature burned into them, and the second, regenerative, the divine Word that erases the Catholic marks of defacement and reintegrates the martyrs' bodies as part of a text into Scripture (and, concomitantly, into Crespin's *Histoire*).[29] The judicial testimony is converted, by the martyrs' insistence and faith, into the repository of the martyrs' identity in Christ; what they have to say there is speech of spiritual significance, expressing all that they ever hope to be. And it is a powerful witness: on occasion, judges weep upon hearing the confessional statements. Antoine Laborie records that at his trial, "tant que je parloy, tous avoyent l'oeil sur moy, et moy sur eux, et en vi quelques uns des plus jeunes qui avoyent la larme à l'oeil". (322) The martyrs do not protest at the requirement of a confession, but rather gladly compose it. Their only criteria are that it be complete and truthful. When supplied with only a half sheet of paper on which to write, they call for more paper, and ever more, creating a book of faith out of their own lives. In the construction of the martyrology, Crespin imitates their struggle to procure ever increasing quantities of writing materials. He does so by retaining the fragmentary nature of their statement. He labels each letter, piece of confession or trial transcription separately, miming the original staccato composition. Antoine Laborie laments that he can only record his confession in fits and starts: "...comme par pièces, la somme de qui en est, selon la mesure de papier et de l'encre que nous pouvons avoir ... j'ay bien voulu escrire" (322-25). The martyrs write copiously, knowing that this confession will be their final offering to God and to the Church, hoping that the paper will speak for them after their tongues have been torn from their mouths. Yet marvels occur. So close is the symbiosis among body, word and Word, that the body miraculously speaks after it has been silenced (just as it continues to do in the *Histoire*). "Le bourreau demanda premièrement la langue d'Estienne Mangin, lequel la bailla volontiers: et après que le bourreau lui lut couppee, en crachant le sang parla encore assez intelligiblement, disant trois fois, le nom de Dieu soit bénit" (172). Pierre L'Escrivain, the oldest of the Cinq Escholiers à Lyon, willingly participates in his trial, attending with joy to the enunciation of his beliefs. But he is perturbed by the court clerk's inattention and failure to transcribe some of his utterances. L'Escrivain protests to the court, requesting that they grant him the right to make a complete statement: "Or voyant que le Greffier n'escrivoyent pas ce que je disoy, mesmement les passages que j'amenoys de l'Escriture saincte, je di alors à l'official, Monsieur, le greffier n'escrit pas ce que je dy, à ce que je voy" (206). We note the relationship between L'Escrivain's statement and biblical Word: "ce que je dy" is, in many of the martyrs' cases, that which Scripture has stated. They do not hesitate to strengthen their statements with scriptural borrowings, so close is their identity to that of Christ (who also experiences a textual resurrection, as his body, ultimately, is only recuperable for the faithful through the book). L'Escrivain volunteers to substitute himself for the court recorder—to engage himself in the actual cast of characters responsible for the requisitoire and his eventual death—in order to see to it that the transcription will be accurate.[30] "Parquoy il vous plaira de me donner de l'encre et du papier, pour faire ma confession, et pour démontrer par passages de la Saincte Escriture ce que je croy et confesse et que je ne dy rien contre la Parole de Dieu" (206). The request is granted, although L'Escrivain's confession is so extensive that he never does entirely finish: his persecutors finally demand that he attest to the portion that he has completed: "Response [de l'Escrivain]. J'en ay bien escrit une partie seulement mais je vous prie de me permettre que je l'achève, et de commander au Géolier qu'il me donne du papier. Lequel me dit, Lisez ce que vous avez escrit" (206). We have the impression, due to the length of his statement, that his book is coextensive with his life; he could go on writing, confessing his faith, forever. This intimate relation between body and book the Catholics seek to sever, here prefiguring the silencing of L'Escrivain's voice which will occur at his death. They reinstate themselves as figures of authority in a drama which has been temporarily usurped by the strength of L'Escrivain's confession, the proliferation of this writing paradoxically made possible by the confinement of his body.

### Corporeal Confession

Writing always occurs, in this collection, under constraint, since writing is the required (yet, paradoxically) jubilant response to the circumstances of imprisonment. Thus, writing is both the expression of physical claustrophobia as well as of spiritual release. Antoine Laborie expresses this dialectic in a letter to his church: "quant à la prison, je ne pourroy déclarer de bouche ni par escrit la douceur, le bien et le contentement que j'ay reçu en icelle. Toutesfois je puis dire à la vérité que je ne fus jamais mieux à mon aise, et selon le corps et selon l'esprit, que j'ay esté et suis depuis mon emprisonnement ... . Je vous ay bien voulu escrire toutes ces choses

... afin que soyez participans de ma joye" (325). He writes not only to witness, but also to urge and to facilitate participation in his experience, attending to both the body and to the spirit. Like Laborie, these men and women seem to want for nothing other than pen and paper while in prison. Nowhere do they express hunger, describe pain or humiliation.[31] This obsession with writing translates into the martyrs' abdication of bodies to be God's instrument, the means by which his Word (oral and written) shall be proclaimed. Three steps will follow this surrender of self and voluntary complicity in their torture. First, they will write a confession. Then, the Catholics will publicly inscribe their punishment upon them. Finally, God will write over that indictment, effacing it by the strength of his Word.

It is essential for the realization of this process that the martyrs record only truth. They attest to this loudly. When asked "Voulez-vous maintenir cela que vous avez escrit" (effectively, "will you cooperate in condemning yourself to death?"), Laborie proclaims, "Oui, monsieur, jusques à la mort, car c'est la vérité de Dieu" (206). They speak not their own words but those which God dictates. And they manifest veracity by sealing the words, placing a spiritual stamp of finality upon them. The term "scelle" recurs constantly, along with "seing;" both indicate a personal stamp, one that would be fashioned of an individual's *devise,* or picture and word motto chosen to convey through symbolic representation the essence of the individual. These stamps would be used to close up a letter or document of importance, and would clearly indicate to the destinator from whom the letter came even before it was opened. Such seals are synonymous with a sixteenth-century conception of personal identity. When the martyrs offer to seal their testimonies, they are making these statements coextensive with who they perceive themselves to be.

Confession converts the martyrs into divine truth, which they validate in their blood. Crespin instructs us that "selon le temps, le Seigneur par sa bonté admirable a redonné à l'église non seulement des fidèles Docteurs pour annoncer sa vérité: mais aussi des excellens champions pour la sceller de leur propre sang" (39). The symbolic seal is made physical through a figure of speech; the martyr Baudechou describes this process: " ... que nous puissions sceller par les cendres de notre corps ..."(386) The speech torn from the tortured body, that speech which respeaks the Word of God, both originates from, redeems and perpetuates the body. Crespin cooperates in this recuperative work, himself intervening once the martyr's death has silenced his voice.

Crespin insists that the martyrs are "conformes" to Christ: "Que les persécutions sont inévitables à tous ceux qui veulent droitement suivre Jésus Christ, et faire vray profession de son Evangile ... que pour participer à sa gloire ... nous lui serons entièrement conformes à sa mort et passion" (327). "Conforme" conveys a notion of actual, conscious self-shaping in order to emulate a model. It has a sense of exactitude and orthodoxy, but possesses very physical, literal ramifications: one's adherence to Christ will be exhibited physically in the body, as though His Word, emblazoned within, should suddenly render the body transparent and the interior Word externally legible: "nous sentons sa saincte parole escrite au profond de nos coeurs en lettres d'or." (36) Thus, when the body is burned at the stake, the fire purifies it in a strange alchemy so that the body is reduced and distilled to its motivating essence: the Word endures. Here, Crespin proclaims the survival of the Word through his human word: a new, textual body as container of the human utterance that communicates divine speech. Crespin operates a sort of narrative resurrection of the body. After the dispersal of Jean Hus's ashes by the Catholics, for instance, Crespin has the last word, to remind the reader that the death sentence was in vain: "Loué soit Dieu," he says in the face of death, "l'indignation est cessée, le père de miséricorde et le Dieu de toute consolation ... a tué en partie par l'esprit de sa bouche ce méchant adversaire ... Amen" (66). He seals their statement through a guarantee of the authenticity of the documents he assembles[32], as well as through his participation in the Calvinist faith.[33] His writing thus becomes a second seal, overlaying the martyrs' completed confession and personal, corporal seal.

This palimpsest effect of speech, and of written word in letters, trials, confessions and narrative accounts underlines the significance of the writing act as testimonial in the *Histoire*. The multiplication of discourses constitutes a solid block of potent words that works to counteract the secular and spiritual arms of the Catholic persecution.

Unwittingly, the Catholics participate in Crespin's redefinition of the verbal order they attempt to impose. For example, the act of condemnation of Jan Hus and Jerome of Prague requires that they wear caps bearing the label "heresiarcha," on which are painted "trois diables horribles" (61). This supposed humiliation and intended condemnation is promptly erased by two factors. First, Hus and Jerome redefine the cap, likening it to Christ's crown of thorns and thus construing it as a sign of glory. Hus says, "le Fils de Dieu mon Seigneur Jésus Christ a porté pour l'amour de moy une couronne d'espines ... pourquoy ne porteroy-je pour l'amour de luy ceste couronne légère" (61). Secondly, when the body is burned, so is the cap, and the representation on it. Paradoxically, the disappearance of the martyr's body entails the disappearance of the representation intended to seal the martyr's indictment. The fire meant to punish Hus instead confirms him; it is, in fact, an unearthly, purifying fire, just as God takes up and converts to his purpose the instruments of all the other martyrs' torture and death: "je voy au feu un autre feu reluire,/ Je voy un feu brusler un autre feu .../N'est pas feu, plus feu que le feu mesme" (vi).

The Catholics constantly attempt to silence the Protestant polemic. The description of the execution of the Calvinists at Meaux illustrates the battle of words; this is a drama in which layers of discourse accumulate, until suddenly a climax is reached, and the final speaker prevails. "Là les bourreaux commencèrent à les lier, comme agneaux destinées au sacrifice. Et pource que ceux qui avoyent les langues couppées ne cessoyent de louer Dieu, et les autres de chanter Pseaumes; les Prestres qui estoyent là comme forcenez, se prindrent à chanter, *O salutaris hostia, salve regina*; et autres blasphesmes exécrables" (172).

Sometimes, images of overlayering describe the dispersal and reassemblage of the martyrs' mutilated. Here, the fragments of bodies function as so many *semes* in a spiritual semiotics; dispersed, the speech they formulate is temporally silenced, but collected and reintegrated in the *Histoire,* they join together to articulate a potent witness to the martyrs' perseverance, even in death. An example of such an overlayering occurs in the account of the Saint Bartholemew's Day Massacre. Marauders separate a young woman from her husband, murder her and throw her in the Seine. Her long hair tangles in the pier and prevents her from floating down the river, so her dead body lies there for three days. Subsequently, the Catholics throw the body of her murdered husband into the river. The Catholics think that they have separated these two by death. But as it is being thrown into the river, the young man's body lands on top of that of his wife, overlaying her and creating a gruesome image of reassemblage. Their reunion constitutes a powerful denial of the Catholic attempt to silence and separate them. Crespin rejoices that "son corps jetté sur celui de sa femme, laquelle il emmena avec soy, et par ainsi le tindrent compaignie en leur sépultre" (707). Other images are more directly evocative of the Catholics' attempt to mark, or write on, the Protestants' bodies, in order to silence the Word that those bodies speak. For instance, posthumous torture patterns the bodies of the Cinq Escholiers à Lyon with an intaglio: "le bourreau, après avoir greffé leur chair nue; et jetta dessus du soufre pulverisé" (314). The bodies of the Escholiers serve as paper, the ink the mark (and agent) of pain. Yet this is merely a superficial inscription, skin-deep only, for it is profoundly contradicted by the confession of Christ indelibly engraved within the martyr's heart: "car nous portons Jésus Christ en nos coeurs, le fils de Dieu vivant: et nous sentons sa saincte parole escrite au profond de nos coeurs en lettres d'or" (386). Occasionally, the persecutors are referred to as "autheurs" (722). The dual connotations of "acting upon" as well as "writing upon" coexist in the sixteenth century usage of the term.[34] Three hundred Calvinists are massacred in Bordeaux and their dead bodies are laid out in rows. The "auteurs" of this devastation strip the corpses, mutilate them beyond all recognition, then cover the sex organs with paper: "après les avoir pillez et despouillez de leurs accoustrements, ils les estendirent ... tous nuds, leur ostant mesmes la chemise, et leur laissant pour toute couverture une feuille de papier à chacun deux sur leurs parties honteuses" (722). Inevitably, these sheets of paper would become stained with the blood of the corpses they cover, recalling the confessions some martyrs wrote in their own blood. The blood of the martyrs seeps up into the paper, "writing" a testimonial of their torture, while the intent of the Catholics had been to cover up the bodily mutilation. A tension exists between the two discourses rivalling for disclosure. Blood reveals truth. The marks of the wounds of the dead martyrs record their ordeal. Crespin registers divine retribution on one of the perpetrators of the crime. In this letter, for instance, his own blood, welling up around him, acts as a mirror, and forces him to recognize his sin, as well as causing his death: "Un des plus ardents à ceste [persécution] ... tost après il fust surpris d'une affluxion de sang par le nez ... C'est un grand cas, de veoir sa teste baissee dans un bassin plein de sang ... Bref ce malheureux ... qui n'avoit peu saouler ses yeux du sang innocent qu'il avoit espandu ... se mira en son propre sang tant qu'il en rendit son ame" (724). Blood (ink) has a memory. It records sins, and writes the evidence of them. Blood is the medium of the martyrs' statements of faith; it writes God's truth. "Car ce qu'on void aujourd'hui prouvenir du sang universellement espars de ces martyrs déclare et conferme ... l'oeuvre de Dieu ... [Ce] sont les marques coustumières que Dieu a donné aux tesmoins qu'il veut choisir et produire en sa cause" (3). Blood is the guarantor of veracity. Crespin uses the image of blood to associate the *Histoire* with the martyrs' own writing: "J'ay trouvé quelquesfois des choses obscures, comme escrites en cachots tenebreux, et souvent de sang que les pauvres Martyrs s'estoyent fait sortir" (3).

Catholic marks of defacement attempt to efface Protestant identity. In the Saint Bartholemew's Day Massacre, minions of the Duc de Guise brutally murder the Admiral de Coligny in his bed. De Guise waits below, but then, wishing to be certain that it is indeed Coligny who has been killed, requests to view the body. The torrents of blood still pouring from the victim's head wound obscure Coligny's features. De Guise carefully wipes the blood from the battered face in order to ascertain its identity. Once assured, he kicks the dead man in the face, again effectively defacing him and obliterating his identity: "Or d'autant que ce coup que [Coligny] avoit receu en la teste, et le sang qui le couvroit empeschoit qu'on le conust ... le Duc de Guise se baissa dessus, et lui torchant le visage avec un mouchoir, dit, je le conoi... puis ayant donné un coup de pied au visage de ce pauvre mort ..."(704). The Catholics seek to turn their Calvinist victims into types of reversed relics, who then receive opprobrium rather than veneration. De Guise embalms Coligny's head and sends it to the Pope in Rome. But Crespin's account counteracts de Guise's intention, recuperating the dismembered pieces of Coligny's body by rehearsing and narrating their dispersal, and by citing Coligny's words prior to, and in, death. He forms a reconstituted epistolary body.

The Catholics attempt in other, less murderous, more subtle, but nonetheless damning ways to distort Protestant identity by layering something over it. Antoine Laborie recounts the persistent attempt by his Catholic judges to trick him into swearing before an image. They attempt to superimpose their reality, beliefs and discourse over his. "Incontinent que je fu entré, l'un des principaux commanda au Greffier de me présenter un tableau, où il y avoit un Crucifix peint, et me commanda de me mettre à genoux. Je respondi, à Dieu ne plaise que je me prosterne devant l'idole, ou créature ... Je me soubmets à vostre commandement; pourveu que l'idole soit ostee de là. Alors il commanda au Greffier d'oster l'image et derechef il me commanda de me mettre à genoux ... Je me mis à genoux. Incontinent il me fit rapporter l'idole pour jurer: ce que voyant je me voulu relever." (321) This attempt to pervert another's expression is illustrative of the many instances of manipulation and distortion throughout the *Histoire*.

### The Sundered Body and Its Return

Crespin insists that the Catholics destroy and disaggregate as much of the bodies as possible.[35] It is somewhat puzzling that the Catholics emphasize the dispersal of the body, since saints' bodies were customarily divided up after the eighth century[36] for veneration at various shrines. What is perhaps helpful in this regard is the Catholic insistence on absolute obliteration of any coherent form of the martyrs' bodies. The bodies are so minutely cut-up and dispersed that any reassemblage would, in truth, be impossible. Even skulls were ground down to dust; fingers were disarticulated at each joint; bodies were reduced to ashes which were scattered far and wide. In a reversal of the Catholic attempt to annihilate the Protestan body and to ensure that it would never return, Catholics at a dinner party several weeks after a massacre found the fractured finger bone of a Protestant martyr in the belly of the fish on which they were feasting. The martyrs' presence returns, synecdochally, as the fish also recalls the resurrection type of Jonas in the whale's maw. "Quelques uns [des corps des martyrs] estoyent dévorez par les poissons, que les Papistes refusoyent de manger et spécialement ayant veu la rivière convertie en sang, et qu'ils entendirent dire qu'on avoit retrouvé, quelques semaines après les massacres, au ventre d'un brochet, en une compaignie de Papistes, le poulce d'un homme."(715)

Through his recuperative technique in the *Histoire* Crespin shows that it is the Word the body displays, that textual skeleton constituted by its discourse, utterances, letters and confessions, that effects a resurrection. Crespin prefigures Christ's final opening of the tombs when Crespin exhumes the martyrs in his text: "Le mal est en cecy ... on a laissé presque *enseveli* la mémoire de tant de morts ... Dieu leur met la plume en la main pour rédiger par escrit ses oeuvres admirables, lesquelles il manifeste par les Tesmoins de sa cause ... "(2) By reading the divinely-motivated confessions, the reader sees, resuscitated before him or her, the absent body in the present text: "revoyans les vivans en leurs responses" (2). Crespin turns the marks of martyrdom, those mutilations effected on the martyr's body, into the insignia of salvation in Christ: "ce que nous avons récité ci dessus, assavoir de pareils effects de la mort de ceux-ci de nostre age, ... sont les marques coûtumiers que Dieu donne aux tesmoins qu'il veut choisir et produire en sa cause"(3).

### An Alphabet of Agony

His writing rectifies the false, deceitful writing of the Catholics: sentences of death and scarring of bodies become statements of eternal life and Christiform stigmata.[37] The body which produces the text from its own corporeal components (blood, tears, bones), and the text as reconstituted body through its epistolary constructions, are the joint poles of the resurrection experience. Images of the confounding of the antagonist's intent prevail in the text. One of the more noteworthy, because concerned with the same preoccupation that obsesses the martyrs (the uses of language and writing) is that of the alphabet of agony, a roll call the Catholics made, in orderly fashion, of the surnames of those about to die: "La pluspart furent sommez au sortir, à mesure qu'on les appelloit par leurs noms, selon le rolle qu'avoit les massacreurs" (721). Crespin creates the reversal of the roll of death into the register of life. He calls out alphabetically the names of those same martyrs.

He asserts their new, present elect existence by and in the Word. His is an act first of recuperation, then of resuscitation. "Ayant recouvrez de quelques personnages délivrés de la main des bourreaux, par une singulière providence de Dieu, les noms de [ceux] qui furent lors massacrez; je les ay icy inséré ... le temps nous fera recouvrer (s'il plaist à Dieu), les noms des autres, afin que la postérité les conoisse ... Et s'il avient que ce grand nombre de quinze ou dix huit cents hommes meurtris en si brief espace dans Lyon demeure ensevelis sous silence, pour cela ils ne laissent pas de vivre d'une meilleure vie qu'en papier ... Nous suyvrons en ce dénombrement *l'ordre de l'alphabet.*"(719; my emphasis) Crespin then mentions the list of names in a tight, textual block, devoid of narrative or commentary. All must be named so that they can participate in the reconstitutive text, a text which both resurrects the martyrs, and whose substance is also formed of them. The mention of "rolle" cannot fail to remind the Protestant readers of the divine book in which God records the names of the elect[38]; Crespin's list is analogous to God's. To confirm the election, it suffices to read, and read again, Crespin's text: "Que tous fidèles réduisent souvent ceci en mémoire"(i). Salvation is the essence of Crespin's textual rendering of the martyrs; salvation is equally proffered to the thoughtful reader: "Si on veut donc d'un vrai proufit joyr,/ Ce n'est assez, et de voyr, et d'ouyr,:/ Car au penser est l'utilité toute." (v) Crespin in fact inscribes in his text the sort of reader he desires, just as the martyrs direct the way in which their confessions are composed and should be read. Crespin also inscribes an anti-reader in the *Histoire*, one who typifies the Catholics and those he anticipates will denigrate his text (" ... irrités contre ce livre." ) Crespin exults in the supreme creative paradox that, were it not for those persecutors who filled the role this anti-reader plays, this text, Crespin's *Histoire*, could not have been written: "Appren-le donc, si par cruel Martyre/ Tu ne mettois les fidèles à Mort/ Nous ne pourrions, sans te faire grand tort/ Mettre en avant ces Recueils pour les lire." (v) Crespin guarantees the integrity of his text against this reader, who would play him false, stigmatizing the anti-reader with the marks of fallen language, a textual wounding of the body. "La corruption se trouvera plustost là où les ordonnances d'icelles saincte parole sont falsifiées, et autres établies à la volonté des hommes." (ii) Thus, two diametrically opposed readers of the *Histoire* are acknowledged within the text proper. One of them reads the confessions of faith in order to strengthen personal faith and actions; the other rereads the works of those he had condemned[39]: "Et vous juges, qui avez condamnez, reprenez, comme par forme de recolement, la Lecture de leurs Confessions." (3) This dialectical play between reader and anti-reader figures the oppositional dialogue that the text transcribes verbatim between Protestant martyr and Catholic persecutor. By juxtaposing the two reader types, Crespin enables the *Histoire* to mime the very legal processes, tortures and condemnations from which it derives its textual history.

Through his arrangement of, and intervention in, the texts he collates, Crespin acts as a facilitating filter for the words and Word contained there. This new text is structured around the powerful symbol of corporeal reassemblage, the rejoining of severed heads, and arms, and thighs in a pattern that speaks a language of pain, and of belief. The text is the body, and that body makes the text.

# Notes

All citations to Crespin refer to the Geneva edition of 1597 (after additions since the first edition of 1554) and appear in parentheses after the citation.

1. For this, and for other reasons, the neglect that Crespin's *Histoire* has suffered is astonishing. This is a book that was widely quoted by contemporaries. Agrippa d'Aubigné quoted some passages verbatim, and reworked others, in his *Tragiques*. The *Histoire* seems even to have played a role in the *culte*; Halkin notes that portions of it were read as part of a worship service. [Léon Halkin, "Hagiographie protestante," in *Analecta Bollandiana*, 68 (1950), 462.] Piaget and Berthoud remind us that "des *Livres des martyrs* , ... on en a fait, au XVII$^e$ siècle déjà et de nos jours, des extraits pour l'édification et instruction des fidèles." [Piaget et Berthoud, 50] In 1950, Halkin noted that the *Histoire* "n'a pas encore d'édition critique, mais une réimpression moderne annotée. (Toulouse, 1885-89)" p. 462; no new impression has appeared to date, and the critical edition has yet to be undertaken.

2. Piaget and Berthoud, 50, observe that "la méthode, s'il y en a une, est fort difficile à préciser."

3. Halkin, 461.

4. Halkin, 461.

5. For instance, chronological order has not been observed. How then does the arrangement of materials procede?

6. Daniel Russell, *The Emblem and Device in Renaissance France* (Lexington, Kentucky: French Forum Publishers, 1986), 160-181.

7. Consult Catharine Randall Coats, "The Devil's Phallus: Humanistic vs. Theological Notions in Béroalde de Verville and Agrippa d'Aubigné," in *Stanford French Review,* 13 (1989): 37-48 and Coats, "Dialectic and Literary Creation," in *Neophilologus*, 72, (1988): 161- 167.

8. However Jean-François Gilmont, in *Jean Crespin, un éditeur réformé du seizième siècle* (Geneva: Droz, 1969), 165, observes that "dans les premières éditions, Crespin est fort discret sur son rôle personnel. A partir de 1564, il utilise plusieurs fois la première personne du singulier pour évoquer des souvenirs vécus."

9. Piaget and Berthoud, 59-61, question whether "Jean Crespin ... malgré ses affirmations et ses protestations de fidélité, n'a-t-il pas redressé, c'est-à-dire, revu et corrigé, arrangé et complété certains textes ... malheureusement, de tous les documents que Crespin a vus passer entre ses mains rien ne s'est conservé."

10. Such as Guillaume Salluste Du Bartas and Agrippa d'Aubigné.

11. *Dabar* in Hebrew signifies both word and act.

12. Gilmont, 183, notes that "il est plus important d'examiner comment Crespin exploite les textes dont il s'inspire ... la comparaison avec les sources utilisées impose une première constation: le message de Crespin lui est propre. Son plan est unique."

13. Crespin, 105. "Ce qui advint en la ville de Paris est digne de mémoire, dont elle est vulgairement appelée l'année des Placars, pour l'histoire qui s'ensuit."

14. Crespin, 38, asserts that through inclusion in his text the martyr will live eternally.

15. Robert Kolb, 87, notes that, indeed, "Crespin ... had a[n] ... appreciative audience prepared for his work by the cultivation of medieval piety."

16. Halkin, 187, notes the impossibility for Protestants to avoid utterly writing in a hagiographic vein: "L'hagiographie protestante n'est pas l'hagiographie catholique, mais les biographies des martyrs appartiennent authentiquement à la littérature hagiographique." I feel, on the contrary, that there is a clear and necessary distinction between the manner in which *vita* (saints' lives) and *acta* (martyrs as testimony) are construed, and that it is in and through this distinction, as Calvinists perceived it, that Calvinist writing aims at incorporating the body only to surpass it and give voice to the Word/word.

17. We see the change in the resurrected body of Christ, at first unrecognizable to those who knew him best, in *John* 20: 14-16 as well as in the Emmaus appearance, *Luke* 24: 13-32.

18. Roland Bainton, *Women of the Reformation in France and England* (Boston: Twayne, 1973), 233.

19. The disciples are viewed as bodily epistles in 2 Corinthians 3:1-3.

20. For instance, Crespin, 170, describes the ville de Meaux not by its physical characteristics but by the imprint of faith upon it: "Meaux peut à bon droict estre mise au premier reng de celles qui en ce temps ont esté participantes de bénédictions et grâces célestes par la parole de Dieu."

21. Crespin, 696, does this to such an extreme as to acknowledge the occasional need to resort to a conventional history to clarify the points he makes: "si quelques fois nous entrelaçons quelques mots de l'histoire parmi, ce sera pour rendre les discours plus intelligibles."

22. I am indebted to Professor Eugene Vance for making me aware of the publications of some members of this school, as well as for his insightful and stimulating comments about "Icons and relics" at the Newberry Library, June, 1989.

23. Persons who evidence concern with the mutual influence of body and language, and whose work I have consulted Elaine Scarry, *The Body in Pain* (Berkeley, California: University of California Press, 1985) and Elaine Scarry, ed., *Literature and the Body* (Baltimore: Johns Hopkins University Press, 1986); Julia Kristeva, *Powers of Horror: An Essay on Abjection* (New York: Columbia University Press, 1982); and Mieke Bal, in Scarry, *Literature*. Other critics whose concerns are in some manner relevant to mine in this study include: Michel Foucault, *Discipline and Punish*, trans. Alan Sheridan (New York: Columbia Press, 1979); Peter Brown, *The Body and Society* (New York: Columbia University Press,1988); Caroline Walker Bynum, *Holy Feast and Holy Fast* (Berkeley, California: University of California Press, 1987); Shoshona Felman, *Le scandale du corps parlant* (Paris: Gallimard, 1980).

24. Scarry, *Literature,* xi.

25. Brown, 194-95.

26. Scarry, *Literature*, xvi.

27. *Ibid.,* 76 and 81.

28. Brown, 120, also observes the significance of volition in the martyrs' suffering and statements: they "belong[ed] not to desire but to the will."

29. The statements of many of the martyrs scaffold their few, frail human words upon the strength of Scripture. I quote from Anne du Bourg's interrogation in Crespin, 472: " ...scavoir s'il est licite d'invoquer les Saincts trespassez. Je vous responds que nous n'en avons aucun commandement par la parole de Dieu. Mais au contraire nous est commandé, quand nous voudrons obtenir pardon de nos péchez d'invoquer le Seigneur par le moyen de son Fils Jésus. Il est escrit au Pseaume 50. Invoque-moy au temps d'adversité, et je te déliveray ... Autant est- il dit en Isaie 55. Joel 2. Rom. 10. Ephésiens 2. Ainsi est dit en sainct Mathieu II. Venez à moy, vous qui estes chargez, et je vous soulagerez."

30. And yet, it is only an apparent complicity. For, as Foucault, 60, notes, "the existence of "the last words of a condemned genre" is in itself significant. The law required that its victim should authenticate in some sense the tortures that he had undergone." But in no way does Laborie's confession (or, indeed, his final words) validate the Catholics; he does not bend himself to accept their judgement, but rather offers his confessions — a protestation of faith — to God. Brown, 31, corroborates this assessment: "Their deaths, therefore, involved more than the triumph over physical pain; they were vibrant also with the memory of a dialogue with, and a triumph over, unjust power." In only one instance, Crespin, 101, do I find any expression of regret or concern: an imprisoned father expresses worry over what will become of his daughter.

32. He makes such statements as, in Crespin, 712, "ce que nous avons à réciter de l'estat de l'Eglise d'Orléans a esté recueilli de l'extraict qu'en donna les jours du massacre un chanoine de Saincte Croix, un homme ... détestant les cruautez de ceux de la religion ... outre plus il nous a esté attesté ce récit très véritable par personnes qui peuvent en parler à la vérité."

33. Sometimes Crespin's conclusion takes the form of a simple statement of fact that is, nevertheless, inflected by the dire circumstances attendant upon it to appear to be God's will: after the murder of Guillaume Gardiner, Crespin tersely adds, 201, "Quant au Roy [who had ordered Gardiner's torture], on dit qu'il mourut 3 ou 4 jours après le martyre de ce sainct personnage."

34. This dual sense of autheur is displayed in French as early as the thirteenth century: "acteor."

35. "Il ne pouvait trouver un tombeau qu'au corps du corbeau, ironisaient les fanatiques qui affirmaient que le cadavre de l'amiral ne pouvoit avoir de sépulture; car il estoit repoussé par l'eau, l'air, la terre et le feu." Pierre Miquiel, *Les guerres de religion* (Paris: Fayard, 1985), 285.

36. Hermann-Mascard, 1975.

37. Bynum describes the phenomenon of Christiform bodies; so too does Camporesi, 1986.

38. De Bèze and d'Aubigné both dwell on the significance of the "roolle".

39. It is surprising that no one has picked up on the l'existence of the anti-reader. Gilmont, 188-189, makes the standard, unnuanced assertion that "Crespin n'écrit pas pour les profanes. Il récuse les lecteurs cherchant quelque vaine curiosité ou le plaisir d'ouir du langage bien orné ... [tout est à] l'importance de sa mission ... écrivant ... pour les Lecteurs réformés."

# Memorializing the Martyr:
# Word, Image and the Emblematic Body
# in Théodore de Bèze's *Icones*

Théodore de Bèze, theological heir to John Calvin as well as his successor in Geneva, demonstrates in his writing an evolution from a secular, humanist formation to a solidly Reformed perspective. His earliest work, a collection of poems written while an adolescent, is heavily indebted to classical sources and influenced by the poetic doctrine and practice of the Pléiade, Ronsard chief among those whom he wished to imitate. In 1550 de Bèze published a play, *Abraham sacrifiant,* which was widely read. In it, de Bèze renounced Pléiade norms and sought to proclaim a Calvinist style of writing, one that would model itself strictly on the revealed Word. The pared-down language and anti-rhetorical stance of *Abraham sacrifiant* move in the direction of the *stylus rudus* of the Gospels. These were de Bèze's only explicitly literary productions; he also published numerous theological tracts (*De jure magistratum* (1576); *Du droit des magistrats* (1574); *Histoire ecclésiastique des églises réformées au Royaume de France* (1580); a life of John Calvin (1564); and a meditational tract (*Chrestiennes méditations,* 1581). *Icones,* a theologically-normative work of which the aim was to complement and extend the work of figures such as Jean Crespin, compilers and historians of the persecution of the Protestant church, was published in 1581. This text has never before received a literary reading. However, its inclusion of emblems, which necessitate deciphering, its self-conscious reference to its author, the musings concerning authorship and authority which are embedded in the text, commend it as a work of multiple dimensions, and not solely of religious exposition. In it, the body is of primary importance: the text itself is a corpus constituted from the images and sayings of martyred bodies.

### Remembering Bodies

Icones, Théodore de Bèze's collection of exemplary confessors, was first published in Geneva in 1581.[1] De Bèze conceives of this book as in some sense complementary to, yet in crucial ways different from, Jean Crespin's *Histoire des martyrs* (1554). Although *Icones* does not specifically term itself a martyrology, some of its aims are very similar. Most importantly, *Icones* is intended to function as a sort of proscenium upon which the theater of ecclesiastical remembrance will be played. The memory of the church (as John Foxe and Jean Crespin also acknowledge) is always, necessarily, reactivated by the rehearsing of key *memento mori*: what are, for Protestants, those textual artifacts constituted by the body and the speech of martyrs and confessors. De Bèze's collection makes use, as does Foxe's, of the original meaning of the term "martyrs": these are witnesses, who may or may not have suffered a violent death. The circumstances of their deaths are, unlike the discussions in d'Aubigné and Crespin, less significant than those of their lives. But, unlike the *vitae* portrayed hagiographically by Catholic writers, for de Bèze what counts most is not the earthly existence of a martyr but rather, uniquely, the speech he there articulates. For it is that word which respeaks the Word. De Bèze refers to Crespin, "le premier duquel a si diligemment escrit l'histoire de la restauration des Eglises ... contenant plusieurs excellantes disputes et confessions, très grandement utiles. Mais encore n'est pas cela suffisant pour nous informer pleinement ... Voyant donc ce deffaut ..."[2] Thus, de Bèze's point of departure arises from a perceived lacuna, a textual absence, as though part of the body were present but not "suffisant" or "plein." This initial "deffaut" prompts de Bèze to present his work not as an attempt at compilation and recuperation (as Crespin defines the project of the *Histoire) nor* as a positing of the polemic potential of tortured bodies (as d'Aubigné proposes), but rather as an attempt at completion, of fleshing out the outlines of the body of the church through the bodies he displays and discusses in *Icones*. Alain DuFour suggests a need on de Bèze's part for representative figuration of these missing bodies: "Des portraits ressemblants pourront ... compléter la connaissance que l'*Histoire ecclésiastique* (1580) donne de leur vie et de leurs travaux." (1) It is important to view de Bèze as one whose treatment of the body in his martyrology is complex and ambivalent. Oddly, this strong Calvinist most resembles John Foxe, the Anglican, especially in his incorporation of descriptive imagery in an apparent attempt to dramatize the word. It seems as though word is subservient to image, although such a statement does not adequately assess their complicated relationship two. It is, regardless, undeniable that a certain amount of textual ambivalence, or of de Bèze's own concern over the nature and intention of his writing project appears in *Icones*: this is manifest from the title itself, which omits the verbal characteristic, privileging the first "Icones," qualifying it, strengthening it and defining it as "portrait": *Icones, vrais portraits des hommes illustres,* presenting the book as a static portrait gallery, one apparently more rooted in *space* than the works of Crespin and d'Aubigné. *Icones* itself is conceived as a fragment, an offshoot from a larger textual body.

Many differences in presentation and effect, both personal and cultic, are evident. As de Bèze himself highlights such comparisons, it is important to recognize the self-perceived singularity of his project. De Bèze's work is problematic when we attempt to situate it in relation to the martyrologies written by Crespin and d'Aubigné in that, while Crespin intervenes to a minimal degree by framing and contextualizing the martyrs he cites, and d'Aubigné grants himself extensive authorial powers in effecting an election of those martyrs he will include, de Bèze permits himself apparent arbitrariness in his selection of material. Some of his figures are not even believers.

*Icones* was a controversial work. By incorporating images, de Bèze opened *Icones* to the charge—quickly levied against him by the Jesuits—of succumbing to the very idolatry Calvinist iconoclasts claimed to abhor. Like the Anglican, Foxe, and significantly unlike the Calvinist contemporaries Crespin and d'Aubigné, de Bèze's work relies extensively on woodcuts; in fact, it is scaffolded specifically on these images (whereas Foxe scatters images throughout his text for illustration or for emphasis, but does not originally intend his work to be one in which word and image intimately interrelate). Therefore, we need to consider de Bèze's *Icones* in two new lights: as a martyrology, and as a book of emblems. These two definitions are not mutually exclusive, although they may at first appear to be so, but rather the schema of the latter informs the former. The correlation of word and image in de Bèze's text is most fertile. *Icones* acts emblematically to construct a living portrait of the self: that of its author, as well as those of the figures it contains. In this way, de Bèze joins the current of other post-Tridentine Calvinist emblem writers such as Georgette de Montenay (*Emblesmes et devises chrestiennes*)[3], but seeks to refine the genre by interpolating progressively a more personal element in his text. Through the selection, ordering and exposition of his material, de Bèze reveals himself, as well as the martyrs and other exemplary figures he claims to portray. De Bèze's Calvinist orthodoxy relaxes here in the direction of increased personal intervention and interpolation. This is a work in which word and image interrelate in what are innovative ways. It constitutes an unusual swerve from a solely confessional focus (and from the majority of de Bèze's other writings), for de Bèze's Calvinist orthodoxy moves in the direction of increased personal intervention and interpretation. Such nascent flexibility regarding word and image comes into play in both theological and non-theological writings by Calvinists during the post-Tridentine period.[4]

*Icones* is composed of three parts. The first is de Bèze's preface, characterized by authorial ambivalence concerning the nature of his project and its reception. The second and largest portion contains martyrs and other figures. This section is divided geographically and arranged alphabetically. The emphasis on locale and careful ordering at first echoes the hagiographic tendency to create a locus in which the saint's body can be contained (reliquary, basilica, shrine), visited and venerated. However, the similarities between John Foxe and de Bèze are more to the point. Both are concerned to elucidate an art of memory which will enable material which was (at least potentially) forgotten to be easily and effectively recalled. Memory is that crucial tool which enables a confession of faith to be spoken. Frances Yates' study on *The Art of Memory,* with its theory of memory theaters, casts light on de Bèze's propensity for compartimentalizing his figures, arranging them in ways evocative of their symbolic content. As Yates has shown, the appropriate disposition of figures placed throughout the zones of a memory theater enables their dramatic reactivation as so many elements of a syntax to be reconstituted by walking through and renaming each element in the memory theater.[5] Thus, place acts not to contain or to localize in *Icones* (as in saints' lives) but rather to abstract concrete figures into patterns of speech.

While most men and women are portrayed by woodcut in *Icones,* quite a few of these woodcuts are erroneously ascribed, and a few are duplicated (one woodcut is used to represent two different martyrs).[6] This helps to explain the rather haphazard selection of visual components. If portraits and engravings are used less for their individual identifiability and more for their role as "place markers" in the space of memory, then this arbitrary distribution of image seems less a problem. The strategy of incorporating woodcuts to represent the figures included is one key to the uneasy relationship between word and image in the text. It is surprising that the woodcuts de Bèze uses as point of departure for his textual meditations are in many cases unreliable as attempted reconstructions of a portrait of the figure. The verbal component is thus highlighted, as one which will convey more information, more accurately. It is immediately evident that word and image are unequally weighted in *Icones.* Along with the woodcuts themselves, there are numerous ekphrastic constructions in *Icones.* De Bèze frequently speaks of an image not existing physically in his text, but created verbally and then adduced as an example to a point made by his prose. This engenders an increased complexity in de Bèze's emblematic text: the word immediately apparent in *Icones* then produces another, textually-embedded image, which is both part of the verbal component and separate from it. It at times seems as though image is valorized in *Icones.* Yet, since this secondary substratum of images is generated by the initial, verbal component, that textually-expressed image finally functions to substantiate the power of the word component of the overarching emblem structure. For instance, singing the praises of Michel de lHospital, instead of quoting certain select and powerful phrases from lHospital's writing or speeches, de Bèze stresses the similarity between lHospital's physical profile and that of Aristotle. De Bèze uses this resemblance to formulate an assessment of character, without basing it upon what lHospital has to say about himself: "Il faut adiouster ceci à sa louange, comme chose fatale, et qui se descouvre sur un médaillon fort ancien, que lui et Aristote Prince de tous les philosophes se ressembloyent tellement que l'image de l'un semble estre frappée en celle de l'autre." (143) This technique of superimposition of images at first seems to elevate pictorial depiction (the "médaillon") as more reliable. However, we note that the medal is nowhere physically present; it is reconstructed by the verbal component, and thus is joined to it to speak *ut pictura poesis*. Additionally, since the recourse to a reference to lHospital and to Aristotle's image was deemed necessary, this serves to further devalue the role of the woodcuts in *Icones*: they are obviously inadequate, since the text must generate other images in order to produce a full description. So, the balance tilts inexorably in favor of the verbal element. It is through the image, but by the word, that martyrs again speak in this text.

After the woodcut comes a meditation in prose, often concerning the martyr's physical appearance, sometimes encapsulating the martyr's final speech or verbal self- presentation. This is followed by a short verse which generally reinforces the prose message. Gisèle Mathieu-Castellani in her study *Emblèmes de la mort* proposes a morphology of emblems to which *Icones* conforms. Emblems generally possess three characteristics: image, verse and prose. They may also be defined by a brief title. Mathieu-Castellani determines that a more cohesive, univalent emblem is one in which the author makes an effort precisely to join the three elements to produce unity of message. The iconography of the image is slavishly reproduced in what is usually the title, verse summation and prose description.[7] As near as possible a mimetic effect is thereby produced, in which no one textual tesserum extrudes from the uniform mosaic established. However, perhaps more interesting for scholars, are those occasions on which the iconography of the image (assuming the image is first perceived and read as most accessible, which Mathieu-Castellani demonstrates is not always the case[8]), is not wholly or accurately reflected in the title, verse or prose. These verbal components may, instead, bring new, perhaps even unrelated considerations to bear on the image, creating distance between word and image. To the extent that the verbal elements add to, delete from, or even contradict the image, these verbal components assert themselves as the privileged agents of communication. While fracturing the organic quality of the emblem, they militate for recognition in their own right.

In *Icones*, both the first two parts of the book (that which properly constitutes *Icones* itself) and the (appended or, as I argue, commenting and concluding) collection of emblems, demonstrate the characteristics of what I have called extrusion: the self-designation of one or more elements, and the singling out, by one part of the text, of another section. Rather than work to create a smooth surface in which word and image can slide together to form a hieroglyph, then, *Icones* acts in two ways. First, it is at times a text that competes with itself: word and image struggle within it for primacy and do not always act in lockstep to produce meaning. This competition mirrors the relationship between de Bèze's words and the words of the martyrs. Secondly, parts of the text create a mirror-effect, reflecting in their structure certain portions of the earlier text. The concluding emblems can indeed be seen to function as a metatext. It might even be argued that the metatextual position of the final commentary conveys the perspective of God onto de Bèze's text, for the final component is theologically normative as well as textually reflective. In this section, de Bèze may be attempting to determine how God would view de Bèze's treatment of the martyrs. In this view, the body of de Bèze as shown in his text is interposed between God and the martyrs' bodies, just as it is for the reader of *Icones*.

### The Self's Body

This complex work is difficult to characterize, even for the author himself. The first indication that de Bèze is having trouble deciding precisely what he wants to make of his work comes in the frontispiece to *Icones*. De Bèze is concerned to supply justification for his writing act. Coming as the successor to the compendious *Histoire des martyrs,* what need might there be for *Icones*? De Bèze finds it in an assertion that Crespin's work was not "suffisant," a surprising claim in light of the extensive documentation contained in the latter. Nevertheless, de Bèze claims that Crespin did not sufficiently fuel the faithful.[9] He intends that *Icones* provide spiritual nourishment. It will be characterized both by its informative quality and by its plenitude. He hopes that the men and women contained within it will be reanimated through their inclusion in the volume so that their word may stir afresh the hearts of the listener/reader; the martyrs will function as "autant d'exemples singuliers et très mémorables." (10) In order for these figures to possess such efficacy, he states that it is essential that his work contain nothing but truth.   Like d'Aubigné, de Bèze excoriates writers of fiction who "nous ayans forgé des contes à plaisir ... ont esté puis après recueillis et baillés de main en main pour véritables ... [et doivent estre] justement condamnés." (3)  It is significant that de Bèze and d'Aubigné, unlike Foxe and Crespin, feel the need to make statements disavowing literary creation, for de Bèze's *Poemata* and d'Aubigné's *Printemps,* written some twenty years earlier, were solely literary compositions.[10] To some extent, then, the martyrological projects contained in both *Icones* and parts of *Les tragiques* exist in a state of tension due to remembrance of predecessor texts.   Their theological tenor is highlighted by these former, exclusively literary, productions.  And it may be that such a memory contributes to the manner in which both *Icones* and *Les tragiques* are written.  In *Icones* in particular, the emblematic nature of the text certainly possesses literary aspects.  The bodies which de Bèze will reactivate as speech thus communicate both a theological truth as well as seek to find ways to legitimize the body as source of a sense of selfhood (that which literature, at its most basic level, expresses).

While de Bèze denies any personal ingression into the text ("j'appelle le Dieu de vérité en tesmoin que je n'ay rien icy forgé du mien,"[11]) he contradicts himself in the next line, demonstrating that the composition of the book is utterly dependent upon his own powers of recall: "j'ay suivi la simple vérité de mes mémoires." (6) He attempts, in other words, to eliminate himself from the text as a determinative factor, but he does not succeed:  in fact, he subverts his own project through his treatment of word and image. Personal references proliferate: "je confesse que je parle en ceste histoire ...; mon intention est ..." (6) Self-denial turns into a paradoxical state of self-expression.[12] His text thus becomes more than originally projected:  the exemplary figures convey God's revelation, while the manner of their presentation and organization may be seen to configure de Bèze's self-revelation, in addition.

De Bèze has good reason for wanting to disassociate himself from his text, for he anticipates criticism: "outre ceux qui s'opposent directement à ce que nous appelons vérité et l'Eglise ... les uns me accusant comme menteur, les autres me chargeant comme partial." (7) In a statement intended to make *Icones* less the production of an individual and more the construction of a confessing community by passing on the responsibility for the completion and enactment of his work to others, he declares: "J'ay finalement essayé de réduire toutes les pièces en un corps, par le meilleur ordre que j'ay peu ... désirant monstrer pour le mieux le chemin à ceux qui pourront mieux dresser cy après un tel ouvrage." (8) These "ceux" strike an odd note, given the reproach of incompleteness de Bèze had leveled at Crespin. The vocabulary of "pièces," "corps" and "chemin" works to create the sense of an organic body, although the use of "réduire," in the sense of "to distill," uncannily echoes the accounts of martyrdoms in which bodies are refined down to their bare bones. The terminology also actually effects a reversal, for it is by changing the order of his terms, by dissolving all the "corps" (of his confessors) into "une pièce," that his own methodology will prevail; whereas he elsewhere claims to borrow pieces from others' works in composing *Icones*, in fact he does not extensively borrow. Rather, he innovates in at least one regard, differing from all other martyrologists[13] by refusing to include material from the distant past or the early primitive church.[14] Instead, he takes these martyrs who have recently expired (he tells us that he avoids including confessors who are still living, for fear of causing jealousy[15]) and gathers them to fashion his own, distinct martyrology. And while de Bèze in the frontispiece modestly states that someone else will come after him to more effectively complete the work he has begun[16], the tenor of *Icones* does not bear out such purported self-effacement: directive authorial intervention occurs everywhere in *Icones*, allowing us to discern de Bèze's personality, as well as the figures he presents for praise and pretext. While he thus seems to present himself, as does Crespin, in the role of editor and compiler, the vocabulary he uses gives the clue as to his real self-perception, for he claims out of disconnected "pièces" to create a "corps", a living body rather than inanimate fragments. This is an exercise of textual resurrection in which he actually plays a prominent part.

Stylistic considerations provide some information in this regard. De Bèze urges himself to write "sans m'esloigner du stile d'une simple et nue narrative, ne cherchant aucun embellissement ... sans m'écarter pour faire de long discours." (10) There are, however, discrepancies between intention and implementation. First, the term "narrative" is a significant selection, as it complicates the concept of a declarative statement, one that would indeed be "simple" and "nue" and factual. A literary component, one with nuances of plot and description, is thereby added. We see this even more clearly when we note that de Bèze recycles in *Icones* verses originally published in the *Poemata*. He now incorporates them as summaries of his presentation of certain martyrs and as components, emblematic *pointes,* in the emblem section of the work.[17] The *Poemata,* repudiated by de Bèze as a vain and frivolous work of fiction, here nevertheless resurfaces, as de Bèze's ambiguous literary signature appended to his religious project. To borrow the critical terminology of Nicholas Abraham and Maria Torok[18], de Bèze's earlier, exclusively literary persona here finds itself "encrypted" within the tomb of the text, as a sort of personal double, like a waxen effigy marking the spot of how de Bèze had once perceived himself. This is a fascinating *mise en abyme,* for it encloses within the text the figures of martyrs living and martyrs dead, figures of de Bèze as writer and de Bèze as (at least avowedly) theological figure. The multiplication of bodies swells the text, gives rise to a multivocity that, for the author at least, is self-contradictory. The vehicle for the communication of the plain speech, the truth-bearing factor, is thus rendered further problematic from within.

De Bèze thus posits both past and present personae of himself in his text, writing different temporal modes of existence into the work as a sort of backdrop to the focus on time, rather than the more typical hagiographical concentration on space, in Icones. His body is therefore presented and fractured and fragmented, while the textual bodies, and body of the text, are, on the contrary, cohesive and entire.[19] Part of the problem for de Bèze in avoiding personal intervention, and a major factor in influencing his progressive involvement in the test, is his desire that his textual figures engage the reader in conversation. The reader would thereby actually hear the reactivated, because textualized, word of the preacher or confessor speaking directly to him or her. De Bèze states that he wants this to be the predominant effect of his collection: "Qui empesche donc, comme par le moyen des livres nous entendons la conception des bons et savans personnages qui avec leur trespas communiquent ainsi familièrement avec nous, qu'aussi par leurs vrais portraits nous ne gaignions ce point de pouvoir contempler, et par manière de dire, *deviser avec* ceux de qui la présence nous estoit honnorable tandis qu'ils vivoyent?" (ii verso; my emphasis). The sticking point is still that of mediation, an issue which Foxe must also resolve. For if de Bèze posits books as those intermediary containers facilitating access to truth, the image contained therein might appear to replicate saints' pictures, relics or holy objects of meditation ("leurs vrais portraicts ... nous gaignions le pouvoir de contempler.") De Bèze can only resolve this problem by finding a way to activate the portraits, to encourage them to speak, and to live in the text, so that the reader will not venerate an image, but rather dialogue with a witness ("deviser avec ceux de qui la présence nous estoyent tant honnorable.")

From the foregoing quotation we can also adduce the strategic significance of the emblem component of *Icones*. De Bèze hopes, by providing both the visual, physical lineaments of the martyr as well as his textual fragments, to summon his potential verbal presence, as though resuscitated, in the text. The emblem requires interpretation, not merely viewing; it must be *read* and not merely seen.[20] The method by which de Bèze resolves his ambivalence over the visual presence of the body is by incorporating emblems, rather than representational illustrations (as does Foxe) in his text. De Bèze explains his use of imagery in his dedicatory epistle "A très-illustre Jacques Sixiesme": "La portraiture, tailleure, et autres telles sciences, ne sont à condamner en elles-mesmes. Si la vive voix touche jusques au coeur les escoutans, on ne sauroit nier, puisque nous ne pouvons ouir sinon ceux que nous voyons, que la présence des personnes ne nous esmeuve fort, voire jusques là que nous révérons les gens d'autorité, encores qu'ils ne disent mot ... " (1) This strategy is complicated, however, by the fact that unlike Foxe and Crespin (and even, to a lesser degree, d'Aubigné) on the whole de Bèze does not *cite* the martyrs' words; rather, he substitutes his *own*, sometimes a paraphrase, sometimes his own formulation, for them. Their speech is presented, if at all, through his mediation and in his idiom. It seems that the martyrs' words have less authority than his own construction. This approach is in clear counter-distinction to other martyrologists (notably Crespin) who quote so abundantly from the martyrs that it is at first difficult to discern a distinct authorial presence. De Bèze quotes no one—except, as is the case with the *Poemata*—when he quotes *himself*. Additionally, while de Bèze claims to give priority to word over image, it is striking how many times in the body of *Icones* he reverses their significance. This raises questions as to what value should be accorded to word and image in the martyrology. The apparent negation of his textual strategy testifies to de Bèze's ongoing ambivalence over, and concern for, the reception of his martyrology. In the narration concerning Jan Hus, for instance, de Bèze alludes briefly to Hus's preaching prowess, but mediates this reference through the awkward image of a goose. He observes that "hus, en langue Bohémienne, signifie une oye. O que le cri de ceste oye a esté aimable ... puisqu'à ceste voix, resonnante plustot du ciel que de la terre, les Chrestiens .. ont esté esveillez." (6) But the signature trait of the representation of a goose is not, in fact, how it looks but how it sounds. The clarion call of the goose acts like a trumpet blast to awaken sleepers. The voice of the goose is likened to something celestial ("plustot du ciel"). The terms of comparison are therefore not visual, but verbal. The image thus becomes something one must go in and through in order to hear the word; it is a vehicle, but the process of interpretation does not end with it. Similarly, reading traverses the body of the martyr, which becomes a transmitter for *Verbum* ("Tu fais par ton travail ... que sans peine,/ Ores nous entendons de Dieu la propre voix"—39) and *verba,* de Bèze's own *copia* as commentary on the motivating figure of the body. For one who claims to place such stock in the divine Word and those human words which magnify its effects, de Bèze seems singularly uninterested in faithfully record-ing the words of inspiration his martyrs uttered.

From an examination of the main section of *Icones,* it would appear that de Bèze has several motivations in avoiding such spiritual stenography. First, the procedure of predecessor martyrologists has been to record slavishly the martyr's utterance, painstakingly transcribing speeches, sermons and letters. De Bèze has already expressed in his preface a desire to ameliorate what he perceives to be the inadequacies of such martyrologies. In *Icones,* he suggests a different methodology. The speaking body will not be recuperated, as in Crespin, Foxe and d'Aubigné, by the compilation of textual fragments. Rather than quote or memorialize through citation, de Bèze hopes to create a dynamic verbal and visual theater through the emblematic body. The words of the martyr will speak through the interpretation and careful reading of de Bèze's tripartite text.

The emblematic nature of the text is one component of de Bèze's project. He desires to distance himself from the bodies as image; in this regard his writing is even more iconoclastic than that of Crespin or of d'Aubigné. He explicitly does not recall the dismembered body through the citation of textual fragments which figure, in the *Histoire des martyrs* and the *Tragiques,* the severed bodily parts of the martyrs. Rather, the body in *Icones* is solely and explicitly a textual body, formed through the emblem. The second component in de Bèze's endeavor is the process of selection, one which is difficult to compare with the almost over-documented texts of Crespin and Foxe, but one which we may constructively compare with the selection of materials made for the purposes of literary creation in *Les tragiques.* A winnowing-out process occurs, and de Bèze himself stands at the center of the choices he makes in constituting *Icones.* While the rationale for the inclusion of some men and women is not always immediately apparent (certain confessors are not even Christian, and some, such as François Premier, actually persecuted Protestants), the choice does make sense to de Bèze himself. His choices construct a pattern that tells much about whom de Bèze admired and why. The manner of narrating the contributions of those men and women he chooses, and those aspects of their lives that he decides to emphasize, adds a second layer to *Icones.* This layer describes Théodore de Bèze — his intellect, his spirituality and his self-conception — and not simply the martyrs. Through his juxtaposition of image with word, and through an authorial selection process, de Bèze provides important clues to his own self-conception. De Bèze may, indeed, in some unspoken way, desire *his* word to attain status equal to the potentially powerful word of the martyrs. This may be why he avoids exact representation of their speech, while he does portray them in two-dimensional woodcuts. The dialogue with the martyrs into which he invites us to enter in the preface is not a viable possibility, when no speech other than his is uttered. The dialogue into which the reader is called is in fact one with de Bèze. Because of his concern that *Icones* be an effective didactic tool, and especially because of his sense of mission in which he feels sure that God directs his choice of materials and dictates their expression, de Bèze himself figures powerfully in his work as a clearly authorial figure, and not merely as editor or transcriber. We then read him into his martyrology as the predominant exemplum there established. Such "reading in" is a practice common to Protestants. Proof of election is the certainty that one's name is "written on the rolls." Protestants are saved by writing and by reading. Indeed, the Calvinist religion is itself a textually-created and -enacted phenomenon. It is predicated, at its origins, on the access of the individual believer to Scripture; in its apprehension, it is an intensely personal literary approach to theology. Thus, de Bèze here stands as the primary confessor of the faith, for it is his word which speaks, commenting on the images of others.

De Bèze's presence in the text is reinforced by the way in which he narrates the martyrs' lives. His customary pattern is one in which a general description in the third person singular is subsequently particularized by an apostrophe made by de Bèze to the martyr. An authorial persona thus develops, since it is clearly de Bèze himself who is speaking and who chooses the manner of his address. Again, Jan Hus' case is instructive. The first, general section describes Hus, foresees his martyrdom (and, significantly, already begins to frame this martyrdom in a narrative way: to "tire à conte" can mean to require that one render an accounting, or that a story is made of the events of one's existence): "Du bras puissant de Dieu juge sévère:/Qui, confermant d'Hus la prédiction, /Te tire à conte et à destruction." (6) Then de Bèze speaks directly and familiarly to Hus, "comme aussi ton histoire monstre/Que peu avant ton départ de ce monde tu as prédit telles merveilles." (6) This ability of de Bèze's to enter into dialogue with the dead indicates that, to his mind, the desired resuscitation of the martyr through the juxtaposition of woodcut with prose account has transpired. The immediacy of the address elides present and past, and conveys the impression that the martyr is capable of responding to de Bèze's statements. The promised dialogue, in this regard, takes place. However, this is not a dialogue that is accessible to the reader. Unlike the participatory reader written into the *Tragiques* and the *Histoire des martyrs,* even though de Bèze has collected material from other sources, and indeed continues to receive and edit material sent by subsequent readers[21], he limits the reader's stance to that of reader, not speaker. The reader is the designated recipient of de Bèze's text, but in no way even a secondary creator of it. Only de Bèze engages in a discussion with the presence he establishes in his text. Also, because we see de Bèze consistently acting this way throughout *Icones,* it is obvious that he has made a selection of those confessors with whom he feels conversation would be desirable. These are not static, two-dimensional models to be emulated; rather, as though he were present at a spiritual banquet, de Bèze has chosen those interlocutors who seem to him to possess "esprit". This is one way to account for the presence of non-confessors in *Icones,* for these are figures whose lives reveal humanistic leanings toward which the academician de Bèze would be favorably disposed, yet some of whom are in no way Christians, let alone Protestants. Again, through the process of selection which constitutes it as a text, *Icones* portrays de Bèze more vividly than the figures it includes. Attempting to justify his inclusion of Erasmus of Rotterdam, for instance, de Bèze interrupts his narration of Erasmus' life to disclose editorial considerations: "néantmoins je faisoy quelque conscience de le renger icy, attendu qu'ayant eu son avis à part en plusieurs choses quand il a esté question de la Religion ... il se rendit avocat d'une très mauvaise cause. Toutesfois puis que les bonnes lettres à leur retour au monde lui sont autant redevables qu'à autre quelconque d'alors, je suis content de lui donner place en cest endroit." (25)[22] The reasons for de Bèze's selection are not always theologically-motivated, but rather arise from personal and subjective preference.

De Bèze also appears in the text on those occasions on which he portrays a martyr through a documentary appendix. To recount the trial and eloquence before death of Hierosme de Prague, de Bèze relies on the letter of a witness to it. He prefaces this, however, with his own statement: "c'est raison d'en ouïr parler un tesmoin, digne de la foy en cest endroit, lequel descouvre à l'oeil la détestable iniquité des juges qui te condamneront." (9) De Bèze does not conceive of his text as a sort of legal brief with which the reader is presented and asked to weigh the merits of each case (as does Foxe). The reader's approach to the letter is already inflected, directed by de Bèze. The term "tesmoin" instructs us as to the significance of the format of these accounts. A martyr is produced by de Bèze as a witness ("tesmoin"). This witness to the truth is then himself attested to by the secondary "tesmoin" whose testimony de Bèze includes (while omitting the actual confession of the primary witness, the martyr). Through inclusion in *Icones,* this secondary witness is witnessed to by de Bèze, and as readers we witness to the integrity of the entire textual entity. But to what are we actually affixing our seal? Not to the witness to God, the act of the martyr, but rather to the phenomenon of multilayered, inlaid witnessing that creates the textual substance of *Icones.* We witness to the constitution of a text rather than the confessional preaching of a word. The martyr's body, point of departure for the theological phenomenon, is telescoped as priority is given to the body of the text itself. De Bèze's concluding emblem, while based on the witness's letter, includes several references to de Bèze himself, establishing him as first, privileged reader of his source. Such references also distract the reader from the martyr: "Quand je li le discours que fait ce Florentin/Puissent les craignans Dieu si bien dire et bien faire/Qu'ils ayent comme toy l'escrit d'un adversaire/En tout lieu tesmoignant leur divine fureur." (17)

Images of de Bèze inscribed *en abyme* in his text situate him in the position of reader: "Lisans les livres de tels personnages et jettant les yeux sur leurs effigies, je suis autant esmeu et poussé aussi vivement en sainctes pensées que si je les voyois encor preschans." (2) They situate him as the essential filter, through which any subsequent readers must pass in order to penetrate the text. The frequent allusion to his act of authorship also establishes an interpretive model with which the reader must first contend before addressing the question of the martyrs' veracity, which seems secondary. De Bèze, as the archetypal reader of his text, peruses materials before incorporating them into *Icones,* rereads them once he has made them a part of his work, and then writes the response that they motivate. All this literary activity on de Bèze's part amounts to an epistolary exchange with the dead. But we are spectators merely, noting de Bèze's reactions from our position on the margins. However, for de Bèze himself, such is his success in revitalizing the confessors that the dialogue he initiates with them is always in the present tense, demonstrating the life he has restored to these figures. Often, present participles proliferate, suggesting ongoing existence and activity. Speaking of Philippe Melancthon, de Bèze asks, "sauroit on trouver homme qui peust te louer selon ton mérite ... toy ... parlant et escrivant avec une perspicuité attrayante." (29)

The frequent references to the phoenix that are found in *Icones* may be interpreted as describing the eternal life conferred upon the martyr through God's recognition and reception of his confession. This memorializing is always dependent on its confirmation by de Bèze himself. Thus, the phoenix is a key image in defining de Bèze's self-perception as one who reconfers life through the medium of word and image conjoined in his text. Indeed, one of the emblems found in the third part of the book is central in this regard: "emblesme VI" defies the executioner to deal the death blow and reminds him of the survival of the phoenix: "On dit que le phoenix vi en mort va reprendre:/Si qu'un mesme bucher est sa vie et sa mort,/Bourreaus, bruslez les Saincts: vain sera vostre effort/ Ceux qu'estaindre voulez renaissent de leur cendre." (248) The significance of this emblem as a sort of textual clue or commentary appears when joined with the second part of *Icones,* where de Bèze himself makes the phoenix-like persistence of the martyrs possible by constituting the book as a sort of memory-theater, albeit subjectively formatted, to display them. De Bèze speaks; it is he who defies the executioner, addressing him as "vous". The emblems mirror the pattern established in the martyrology section of *Icones*: they display the same format of woodblock, prose description, and a final, moralizing *pointe* which is invariably written in de Bèze's voice, with an address to a figure in the emblem as "vous". Frequently, the link between picture and *pointe* is very tenuous. The mediatory quality of de Bèze's poetry is thereby emphasized, attesting to a phenomenon similar to that of the second part of the book: de Bèze's authorial persona is everywhere evident.

Another important way in which de Bèze appears in *Icones* is in the role of a reader of Scripture. It is not at all unusual that a Calvinist theologian should present himself in this way; what is striking is the at times disconcertingly skewed rendering — from the standpoint of objective adherence to the words of the Bible, the plain style de Bèze advocated in *Abraham sacrifiant,* his theo-poetic manifesto — that he performs of the portions of the Bible grafted onto his text. Supplementing the account of Pierre Bufler's life with an example from the Bible, for instance, de Bèze declares that "sa maison, semblable à celle d'Abraham, fut toujours ouverte aux pauvres, et sa femme, comme une seconde Sara, secondoit le mari en ausmosnes et visitations des pauvres." (48) This is, however, a false simile.   It effectively generates a subjective "reading into" the biblical text.   De Bèze feels empowered to expand and extend Scripture, creating a mini-narrative from it for his own purposes.   For nowhere in *Genesis* is Abraham explicitly portrayed as one who provides for the poor, nor is Sara described as an almsgiver.[23]   De Bèze appears, then, as a reader with his own agenda, one who has just performed a sort of preemptive strike on the most venerated model of writing.   De Bèze intends to impose his own reading on the Bible, as well as dictate the correct interpretation he expects his reader to arrive at in reading *Icones.* De Bèze's inflected earlier portrayal of Bufler prevails, but in a problematic way:   if the biblical example is recognized to be deliberately distorted, de Bèze's depiction of Bufler can be seen as prejudicially biased.   By reading it and not analyzing it critically, the reader is complicit with de Bèze's view of *Icones.* This directive tendency also appears in his narration of martyrs' lives, where de Bèze is capable of similar distortions or even omission of elements.

De Bèze doesn't really tell us much about his *Icones.* He hardly reproduces their verses (in not one instance does he cite directly, and only rarely does he paraphrase).   Only once does he transcribe a testimonial document.   We need to determine, therefore, to precisely which elements de Bèze does grant the reader access. What impression does de Bèze want the reader to retain of the lives he records?   What does de Bèze see as the ultimate exemplary quality of *Icones* when, frequently, not enough information is provided so that the reader might come to know the martyr's life well enough to emulate his existence?   Indeed, *Icones* shows a tendency either ·toward generalization — near abstraction — of the martyrs' lives — or else extreme particularization.   De Bèze selects individual episodes that speak to him alone, the tenor of which he does not succeed in conveying (or does not want to convey?) to the reader. When we recall the intricate hagiographic genre that had flourished to promote the Catholic cult of the saints, and the manner in which readers pored over these lives in order to assimilate and emulate them, committing every little detail to memory, we see the extreme difference of de Bèze's martyrology. De Bèze differs also from the Calvinist martyrologies. Crespin relies on testimonials, perhaps in order to set his work up in solid opposition, in a negative generic parallel, to the cult of the saints[24], while d'Aubigné explicitly and consistently devalues images, in contrast to de Bèze's ambivalent use of term here.

### Downplaying the Body

We have already noted de Bèze's intention to create a new form of martyrology. His innovation in methodology does not consist merely in an elimination of others' testimony or in a refusal to record the actual speech of the figures he portrays. Rather, it consists chiefly in the *addition* of his *own* witness, perspective and words, the penetration of a subjective consciousness structuring and informing both *Icones* and its reception. It is significant in this regard that, unlike Crespin and even Foxe, de Bèze does not use testimonial in its raw state. He does not incorporate unprocessed documents, but rather speaks of that process which constitutes the text as a sort of *digestion* (thereby referring to the texts in terms relevant to the body): "[les martyrs] nous ont si peu laissé des tesmoignages bien couchés et bien digérées, par lesquels suivant le fil des années, l'estat dicelle se puisse entendre et bien cognoistre." (2) One of de Bèze's concerns is that other martyrologists have not sufficiently authenticated the documents they include. He describes saints' legends being transmitted bodily to a multitude of recipients ("nous ayans forgé des contes à plaisir, qui ont esté puis après recueillis et baillés de main en main pour véritables ... [qui doivent estre] justement condamnés." 3) It is surprising, therefore, that this concern for veracity and his intention to establish a definitive, canonical collection of martyrs should be expressed in such a personal fashion, in which the reader's apprehension of the contents occurs not in a first-hand experience of the pretext but rather through de Bèze's discussion of the contents. The tension engendered by de Bèze's assertion of the documents' authenticity ("je n'ay rien mis en avant que bien attesté," 6) and his avowed methodology, which is pinned on a purely individualistic validation ("mais au contraire j'ay suivi la simple vérité de mes mémoires, soigneusement recherchées et attestées," 7) makes him the exclusive generator and guarantor of his text. He thereby dismisses the martyrs' bodily existence and verbal formulation of its assurances of truth.

One result of this subjective, selective approach to the data of the martyrs' lives is an increasingly schematic, formulaic presentation. It is as though de Bèze's didactic aims cooperate with his desire for self-expression: at the same time that he intervenes in his text, he devises pithy formulae to describe his martyrs' lives. Unlike the hagiography, he does not present, as it were, a genre painting of the martyrs' daily existence.[25] (Significantly, the emblem is not a representational, but rather a symbolic, form). And unlike Crespin, de Bèze does not seek to convince the reader with excessive documentation. Rather, he offers a concise appraisal of the martyrs' merit. The advantage of de Bèze's methodology is that it is easily retained, being nearly mnemonic in its simplicity. For instance, speaking of Paul Fagius, a minister in Strasburg, de Bèze sums up: "Fagius .../Par presches, par escrits, par foy vive il surmonte/L'erreur, le temps, la mort: et vit dessus les cieux." (56) The extreme concision of such appreciations recalls the frontispiece of the *Abraham sacrifiant* in which Abraham's torment over whether or not to sacrifice Isaac is summarily dismissed to retain only what to de Bèze seems essential: "Abraham a creu à Dieu, et il luy a esté reputé à justice."[26] This strategy moves in the direction of the denial of the body. What counts is the manner in which the life of the believer has achieved spiritual conformity to Christ's will; any anguish or hesitation the body might have initially undergone is not significant. This is in direct contrast with the hagiographic treatment of the body as described by René Aigrain, which the care for the body is of utmost importance: "les martyrs eux-mesmes ... sont guéris d'ordinaire dans leur prison des suites de leurs tortures, ... par le Christ ..."[27] For de Bèze (and the other Calvinist writers), the body as body is not important. This may be why, in de Bèze's discussion of confessors and martyrs, he almost never describes the actual torments endured by the martyr's flesh.[28] His treatment of the body also differs from that of Crespin and d'Aubigné who dwell on bodily torment in order to show its conversion into inscription and text. But it is like Crespin and d'Aubigné in that *Icones* focuses on the word which saves, rather than on the unenduring flesh. By eliminating Abraham's personal drama and Fagius' death throes, de Bèze devalues the hagiographic model of body as theophany. For de Bèze, the body is negligeable. Like a component in an emblem, it is something to be set in relation with other elements in order to be interpreted, or acts as a medium to be traversed in order to experience a spiritual awareness, but it is not a bearer of truth.

The disadvantage of de Bèze's "quick study" of the martyr's life is that, unlike the hagiography which provides a cozy, quotidian chamber into which the reader may enter and make herself comfortable, and unlike Crespin and Foxe's compilations which act legalistically, presenting ample documentation for individual perusal and assessment, de Bèze allows no one but himself to weigh the merits of each martyr's case. *Icones* requires an utter suspension of the reader's prerogatives, an abdication of them to the supreme author, de Bèze himself. De Bèze's problematic relationship with the body is intensified when, having obscured the bodies of the martyrs, he spotlights his own body. His textual production arises from a bodily experience of his own. Here, de Bèze's body becomes that surface upon which God acts out his will, a register for divine efficacy, but, first and foremost, the pretext for what is in fact fairly extensive autobiographical display: "Il y a environ deux ans, que Dieu m'a faict la grace d'habandonner le pais auquel il est persécuté, pour le servir selon sa saincte volonté: durant lequel temps pource qu'en *mes afflictions* diverses fantaisies se sont présentées à mon esprit, j'ay eu mon recours à la parolle du Seigneur ... la parolle duquel est toujours accompaignée de l'effect" (48; my emphasis). De Bèze's sick, supine body, the site of divine inspiration, is actually a body that enters into intertextual dialogue. Such intertextuality, we have already noted, is echoed in the format of *Icones,* which includes a section of metacommentary in the third part. Here, as he reads in bed, de Bèze experiences the urge to write from reading the words of others. His postulation of divine inspiration thus seems subordinated, perhaps annulled, by the syntax of this development which logically privileges the following final argument. "Lisans donc les histories sainctes avec un merveilleux plaisir et singulier prouffict, il m'est pris un désir de m'exercer à escrire en vers tels argumens." (49) Rather than yield itself to be God's instrument (rather, that is, than suffer the same treatment as de Bèze inflicts on the martyrs' bodies in *Icones),* de Bèze's body seeks to strive to prove itself in writing ("désir de m'exercer").

This personal authorial assertion is further conveyed by the fact that, while the prose segment which follows the woodblock is somewhat lengthier than the concluding verse section, the prose segment is usually less directive and more neutral in its wording than is the verse section. And it is the verse component that occasionally includes portions of de Bèze's *Poemata.* With few exceptions, all the verses are written by de Bèze (he does transcribe one or two Latin verses) and are more self-consciously *literary* than theological. They include numerous occasions in which de Bèze speaks for himself, uses more inflated rhetoric than in the prose passages, and is more biased in his delivery of the verses. Stylistically, they are more polished. And, on occasion, the verse section is so clearly the preferred avenue for de Bèze's personal intervention that it itself may intervene, interrupting the more neutral, narrative prose flow, physically imposing its status as privileged commentary. This is the case with de Bèze's discussion of Pierre Viret. De Bèze here first celebrates the received wisdom concerning three great Reformers, paraphrasing it thus: "le commun proverbe célébroit le savoir de Calvin, la vehemence de Farel, et l'éloquence de Viret." (127) He then interrupts this viewpoint to express a personal appreciation of Viret in verse. He paraphrases the above prose, then directs its reception: "France si le savoir,/Le zèle, le parler de ces tesmoins te touche,/Et te rejoint à Dieu, tu *peus salut avoir:*/Sinon, de ta ruine approche ça le terme,/Estant de ces trois ci le tesmoignage ferme." (127) He proffers salvation if one favorably receives the words of these men (thereby guaranteeing salvation to those who approve *Icones,* in which book these redemptive words are contained): "Tels sont pour vrays les miroirs où l'on veoit/Le beau, le laid, le bossu et le droict./Car de qui Dieu tasche accomplissans sans feinte/Comme Abraham, la parolle tressaincte/ ... Il en aura pour certain une issue/ ... Meilleure encore qu'il ne l'aura conceue." (113) The way to "tasche accomplir" is by reading *Icones*. The prescription for salvation is here conveyed in verse, and verse is elsewhere highlighted as a more individual, interpretive form of communication. After interjecting his judgement on how Farel, Calvin and Viret should be heeded, de Bèze resumes with a prose narration.

De Bèze also asserts himself by framing each martyr's account with his own introduction, instructing the reader why and how to proceed: "c'est raison d'en ouïr parler un tesmoin, digne de la foy en cest endroit, lequel descouvre à l'oeil la détestable iniquité des juges qui le condamnèrent." (9)  The appropriation of the martyr to his own idiosyncratic purposes is actually licensed by the martyrs' accounts wherein they adopt their own mentors and models to emulate as suits the occasion: one confessor, on trial, "tombant sur le propos de Jean Hus bruslé auparavant, il l'appella homme de bien, juste et sainct personnage." (14)  He uses Hus, his predecessor in martyrdom, as an example, thus inscribing *en abyme* de Bèze's very methodology in the book.

Another example of de Bèze inserting a personal perspective can be found in his choice of vocabulary when he composes poetry in honor of François Vatable, professor of Hebrew at the University of Paris.  De Bèze realizes that Vatable, who was not a Christian, is a questionable choice for inclusion in *Icones*.  Yet de Bèze recognized Vatable for the contribution he made to the philological treatment of these languages—Hebrew, Greek— necessary to study the Bible. It is interesting, then, that in de Bèze's verse tribute to Vatable, he employs a classical vocabulary rather than one with Christian overtones.  Specifically, he substitutes the term "ciel" where one would expect to read "Dieu": "Heureux l'homme savant qui les autres avance!/Mais très heureux celui qui ses prochains dévance/Et qui court vers le ciel." (139) He shows the influence Vatable has had on him by using his textual body to display Vatable's signature.

De Bèze can be seen as an active reader and interpreter of the text he composes.  The mosaic of its components—actual lives, as well as the collection of woodcuts gathered from all over Europe, and the group of emblems—is carefully crafted in accordance with the views of one individual author.  Indeed, the effacement of the martyrs' bodies is necessary in order for de Bèze to write.  He speaks of the martyrs, but it is the absence produced by their death that generates his text. "Ta mort montre suffisamment que ta vie est digne de louange." (19) Their bodies can only be recuperated through his text.

It may be that de Bèze, in this way, hopes to dramatize the significance of speech over image. One manner in which this is evident is his strategy of reversing images, thereby negating their effect uniquely as image, and focusing on the word. For instance, he states that "toutesfois la *fumée* débat fut le chemin à la belle *lumière* de la vérité" (22). Here, the image of smoke yields to light and clarity. Elsewhere, he stresses the incompleteness of image unanimated by word: "ici tu voids *pourtraict à moitié seulement ...*" (26; my emphasis). In *Icones* de Bèze certainly praises iconoclasts for annihilating "les idoles du peuple [qui] sont en or et argent, ouvrages de mains d'hommes." (108) He recounts, for example, the story of Jean de Meaux who "poussé par un mouvement spécial du Saint Esprit ... sortit de sa ville un soir, et alla rompre et abattre les images d'une chapelle." (167)

### The Emblematic Presence

The Jesuits accused de Bèze of himself practicing the very idolatry he condemns. Yet de Bèze does not conceive of his *Icones* as idols, because the powerful authorial presence in *Icones* works to initiate a dialogue between de Bèze and his martyrs. This verbal interaction exalts the potential for speech rather than the veneration of images (even if it is only ultimately efficacious for de Bèze himself). De Bèze includes woodcuts combined with tales of the martyrs to cause word and image to conjoin to produce a presence with whom he may converse. These images are never predominant, but rather act as accessories in the resuscitative alchemy de Bèze performs. Image may inform as to the veracity or status of the word, but it is the handmaiden of the word, and not totality in itself: "jamais les bruits et remuements ne l'étonnèrent, ainsi il demeuroit toujours constant et *de mesme visage ...* sa voix estoit *douce, ouverte, resonnante* et *plaine de maiesté*: sa *contenance* bien dressée." (15) The martyr's inner strength is shown both in the words he utters as well as in his mien and demeanor. Similarly, de Bèze uses both body and speech to create a stronger impression.

Robert Kolb notes, regarding Rabus' martyrology, that "the woodcuts serve, but remain secondary to the printed text, as is perhaps fitting in a chronicle of the Word of God."[29] In the emblem commentary on *Icones,* de Bèze specifies that image is a correlate of the word, but the word is accorded a more dynamic status. *Verbum* is the prime mover, "cause," while images only portray word, "effect:" "O lecteur, il me semble/Que par l'effet, qui au pourtraict ressemble,/Suffisamment tu lis leur nom ici." (268) The image de Bèze describes in this particular instance, a circle of serpents, is in fact abolished by the power of the Word: "Mais Christ ... /Va depeçant ce rond venimeux ici/Par le trenchant de sa vive parole." (268) De Bèze's method is even more extreme, in that the printed text is surpassed: the conception of *Icones* as text is superceded by the voice we hear, that of de Bèze engaged in dialogue with the martyrs. Just as the divine Word animates the text of the Bible, so does de Bèze initiate speech within his text. Were he a less assertive, vocal author, the martyrs might not be called upon to respond to his constant questioning. Thus word, image and authorial commentary combine systematically in *Icones* in a strategy designed to avoid the pitfalls a Calvinist would perceive in the veneration of saints. The presence restored to the martyrs always prevails over any imaged representation of them. In addition, in the construction of the emblem section (as in the first two parts, wherein the martyr's portrait is not always accurately ascribed and is limited often to a sort of generic sketch,) the link between picture and *pointe* is invariably extremely tenuous. The mediatory quality of poetry in qualifying the relationship between the two and making them readable is thus very evident. An example is Emblem 18 in which is seen a house upon which winds from all angles are blowing. The house's windows and doors are locked. The lesson to be learned is not immediately obvious from the image, so a specification is necessary. This clarification is given in verse. "Cela devroit apprendre à qui s'estime sage/De fermer à Satan et l'oreille et les yeux." (258) No iconographic tradition has been followed here to create an accessible image; wind is not a commonly-understood symbol of Satan. Word is needed to explain image. In the emblem section, de Bèze also restores presence, or confirms the validity of, his readers, putting them through the same process experienced by the martyrs in a textual reversal of life into death: "Aussi toy qui sans fard aimes le Christ ardemment,/A la fin de tes jours commenceras ta vie." (241) Elsewhere the threat to the body is explicit: if effective reading is not made of *Icones* ("si conte tu n'en tiens"), Christ will be "[la ] mort" of the reader. (252) René Aigrain characterizes hagiographies as accounts which insist on visually portraying the resurrected body: saints are "miraculeusement ressuscités en vue de supplices plus cruels ... ainsi saint Paphnuce, après avoir été plusieurs fois rendu invisible par l'ange qui avait remis en place ses intestins ... est ressucité."[30] Resurrections of the martyrs are not depicted in Protestant accounts, but they are textually-assured. Here, de Bèze's resurrection of the martyr is a verbal phenomenon. He elides the body in this endeavor. The abstract symbolism of the image component of the emblems is counteracted by the vivid bodily descriptions of the operation of the word. In emblem three, for instance, the image is geometrical and unclear without the verbal apparatus; it is a circle with a square inside it. But the verse describes a walking body: "de marcher rondement ayes toujours envie/En ton estat aussi tien le pas asseuré." (243) The ultimate effect is to use image and body to move beyond them to word and speech. As he asks rhetorically in his verse on Michel de lHospital, "Mais qu'avons-nous besoin de tableau .../En lHospital tu vis et fais ta demeurance." (144)

Word and image are integral parts (albeit unequally weighted) of de Bèze's project in *Icones*. Emblem Thirty-five portrays a bishop seated in his *chaire,* bedecked with mitre and crozier, turning toward the altar on which stands a miniature, *mise en abyme* representation of himself: a tiny bishop raises two fingers in apostolic blessing, mimicking and confirming the posture of the bishop in the *chaire.* The pygmy bishop stands in the location that the Host would customarily occupy at the communion table, demonstrating de Bèze's Calvinist perception that idolatry, the worship of an image or of a body as sacred, has replaced the necessary focus on Christ, the *Logos.* The notion of self adoring an other who himself images that first self perverts the whole sense of Calvinist worship, which is to be directed beyond the self toward the transcendent Other. The emblem's verse states, "Evesques et Prelats,/Vue qu'idoles vous estes,/Je ne m'ebahis pas,/Que faciez tant de cas/Des idoles muettes." (277) De Bèze's martyrs in *Icones* are deliberately the opposite of the heretical conception contained

in the foregoing anti-Catholic emblem. Because word and image
are joined, they are not "muettes;" the "parole" prevails. The body
is employed in *Icones* for the function of labelling or designating.
Once the identity of an individual has been ascertained, de Bèze
moves beyond that representation to determine the significance of
that figure's life: his verbal confession surpasses the confessional
posture of the body. Such is the case with Martin Bucer: "Tel
estoit le visage de Martin Bucer, descouvrant une modeste gravité.
Icelui ayant esté tiré des ordures de la moinerie par la vive voix de
Luther ..." (52) The key for de Bèze is the extent of the body's
responsiveness to the Word ("de vive voix"), and to his word which
probes the potential of the image to develop it verbally. The body
of the church is similarly responsive to the word of the portrait de
Bèze animates: "[Gaspar] Hedio .../Strasbourg ... te [donne]
l'honneur/De l'avoir à son Christ par ta voix mariee." (57) Writing,
the textual expression of the word, possesses the supreme power:
"en escrits, par foy vive il surmonte,/L'erreur, le temps, la mort et
vit aux cieux." (56) The body portrayed in the image or portrait
(and the focus is particularly on the face) does not generate the
word, but rather its lineaments conform to the word's specifica-
tions: "sa noblesse a commencé en Hus par plusieurs vertus
excellents, dont son visage vénérable semble avoir donné quelque
tesmoignage." (60) The role of the emblem section of the book
reinforces this point, for it seems designed to clue the reader into
recognizing that the previous portions of the book are therefore
not limited to portraiture, but are actually themselves emblems as
well: woodcut, verse and prose. These consequently function in a
syntactical manner, as word, rather than as static depiction.

The discussion of Jean Calvin in *Icones* is particularly revealing
of the manner in which de Bèze causes body and word to interrelate, but ultimately privileges the latter. His portrait of Calvin is a
bodily image in woodcut only; the majority of his development
concerns Calvin as a verbal entity, a producer through his bodily
existence, of crucial texts. For de Bèze, Calvin's significance is in
the correct alignment of his word in relation to Scripture, to the
Word, as manifested by his textual productions. "O Calvin ... de
cela soyent tesmoins, premièrement tes livres qui vivront à jamais
... dressez avec un tel jugement, de si solide érudition, et d'un stile
si beau, que l'on ne sauroit trouver homme qui jusques à présent

# Notes

1   The text from which I have worked is Simon Goulart's French translation of de Bèze's Latin original.

2   Théodore de Bèze's *Icones, les vrais portraits des hommes illustres,* Alain DuFour, ed., (Geneva, 1580), 8. All subsequent references will be to this text.

3   See the discussion of Georgette de Montenay's emblems in Daniel Russell, *The Emblem and Device in Renaissance France* (Lexington, Ky.: French Forum Publishers, 1985), 91.

4   Catharine Randall Coats, *Subverting the System: d'Aubigné and Calvinism,* (University of Missouri: Sixteenth Century Studies Press, 1990).

5   Frances Yates, *The Art of Memory,* (London: Routledge and Kegan Paul, 1966).

6   "C'est ainsi que l'édition de 1581 contient un portrait de John Knox complètement différent de celui des *Icones* de 1580: une gravure que l'on avait pu exécuter d'après un portrait authentique, alors qu'en 1580, ne voulant pas laisser l'évocation d'un homme aussi important que Knox sans illustration, les réalisateurs du livre s'étaient résignés à placer sous son nom un portrait imaginaire, d'un homme avec une longue barbe." *Icones,* 2.

7   Gisèle Mathieu-Castellani, *Emblèmes de la mort,* (Paris: Nizet, 1988), 39.

8   *Ibid.,* 49. "L'image conserve son pouvoir de séduction."

9   Although Crespin feels that he has adequately fulfilled his role: "le mal est en cecy ... on a laissé presque ensevelis la mémoire de tant de morts précieuses, qui deussent estre à son Eglise comme guidons et enseignes de sa vertu ... en somme, qui voudrait contempler la condition et l'estat des fidèles de l'Eglise chrestienne ... [mes livres] nous le figurent ..." Jean Crespin, *Histoire des martyrs,* (Geneva, 1564), 2-3.

10  Catharine Randall Coats, "Dialectic and Literary Creation," in *Neophilologus,* 7 (1988): 161-167.

11  Alain DuFour, introduction to *Icones,* 6.

12  This is, of course, probably unintentional on de Bèze's part. He probably never is aware of just how saturated with self his text is. To his mind, his

memory is not the subjective screen the twentieth century perceives it to be, but rather is directed by God. Thus, what de Bèze remembers is that which God intends to have remembered. I am not claiming, therefore, that *Icones* is in any sense a conscious self-construction. It is simply that polemic purposes (although he at first denies possessing any, claiming to write "sans toutesfois aucune passion particulière" 7) have galvanized de Bèze into an assertive, obvious role in his text: "je confesse que je parle en ceste mémoire, non point comme neutre, ains comme estant du costé de la Religion." (6)

13  For instance, we may contrast with *Icones* the martyrologies of van Haemstede and Rabus.

14  He claims that other martyrologists err in basing their witness solely or chiefly on non-contemporary exempla: "... qui pourra suffisamment exécuter tant d'excellens personnages qui ont esté en l'Eglise chrestienne depuis le temps des Apostres, et cependant nous ont si peu laissé des tesmoignages bien couchés et bien digérés, par lesquels, suivant le fil des années, l'estat d'icelle se puisse entendre et bien cognoistre." (2)

15  de Bèze, *Icones,* 6.

16  *Ibid.,* 7. "... ainsi comme préparant la matière à quiconque estant plus éloquent que moy, pourra mettre le tout en telle forme qu'un si sainct et digne subject le mérite."

17  DuFour, introduction to *Icones,* 8. "Dans les *Icones,* Bèze avait repris, pour certains personnages, des épitaphes latines qu'il avait publiées dans ses précédents recueils de *Poemata.*"

18  Nicholas Abraham and Maria Torok, *The Wolf Man's Magic Word,* trans. N. Rand, (Minneapolis, Minn.: University of Minnesota Press, 1986).

19  We contrast this with the portrait of the "corps du saint" offered in Brigitte de Cazelles, *Le corps de sainteté,* (Geneva: Droz, 1982), in which, in chapter one, "Le corps fragmenté," she insists on the necessary fragmentation of the saint's body: "le corps fragmenté, c'est cet éclatement positif, cette dispersion bienfaisante, ... c'est la victoire, par la commémoration narrative et situelle, sur un corps décomposable ..." 75.

20  Daniel Russell, *The Emblem.* See the valuable final, theoretical chapter, "The Emblematic Process".

21  "Je prieray instamment tous ceux à qui ce mien dessein ne desplaira point, qu'ils m'aident à le poursuivre, en m'envoyant au moins les vrais pourtraicts de ceux qu'ils estimeront dignes de la louange donnée aux autres." de Bèze, *Icones,* 3.

22  Another section which is treated similarly is that on Beatus Rhenanus.

23  Abraham welcomes the three angels, but that is a different matter.   In
    addition, the Bible does not describe these visitors as poor, but simply as
    travellers.

24  Robert Kolb, *For All the Saints: Changing Perceptions of Martyrdom and
    Sainthood in the Lutheran Reformation,* (Macon, Ga.: Mercer University
    Press, 1987), 40.

25  See the discussion of the hagiographic genre in René Aigrain, *L'hagiographie*
    (Paris: Bloud et Gay, 1953).

26  Théodore de Bèze, *Abraham sacrifiant,* ed. crit. Keith Cameron, (Geneva:
    Droz, 1967), 1.

27  Aigrain, *L'hagiographie,* 148.

28  *Ibid.,* 145-146.   Again, contrast with Aigrain who notes repetitiveness and
    accumulation of torture details as one characteristic of hagiographies.

29  Kolb, *For All the Saints,* 8.

30  Aigrain, *L'hagiographie,* 148.

# Text, Torture and Truth in Agrippa d'Aubigné's *Les tragiques*

Théodore Agrippa d'Aubigné, once a student of de Bèze in the Genevan Académie, was the author of several literary works. His *Les Printemps* was a youthful collection of poetry characterized by adherence to Pléiade poetic standards and the use of Petrarchan motifs. Upon his conversion to Calvinism, he renounced such a poetic endeavor in his epic poem in seven books, *Les tragiques* (not published until 1616, although begun in 1576), in which poetry was subordinated to the exigencies of theological truth-bearing. The hallmark of d'Aubigné's subsequent writings is his consistent interweaving of religious concerns and literary technique, from the polemic pamphlet *La confession du Sieur de Sancy* (written in 1599; published in 1660) and satirical novella, the *Avantures du Baron de Faeneste* to his autobiography, *Sa vie à ses enfants* (1630) and subtly revealing *Méditations chrestiennes* in which he uses Scripture as a pretext to talk about himself. D'Aubigné's intense self-awareness as an author adds particular interest to his writings since, as an ardent Calvinist, he should have been expected to conform more strictly to antifictional proscriptions: non-exegetical work was not encouraged by the Genevan authorities, yet d'Aubigné persisted in creating works in which an authorial awareness abounds. Thus, in the *Tragiques,* d'Aubigné situates his *own* body in the text in relation to those of the martyrs; he writes himself and his reader into a textual space of ensured election. Writing, which incorporates the body, becomes an assurance of salvation, the zone in which reassemblage and resurrection occur.

## The Rhetoric of the Body

Agrippa d'Aubigné's *Les tragiques* is a text in which the torments suffered by the body serve as point of departure for textual inscription of life, death and resurrection. It is a work in which we find developed an original strategy for writing about lives. It creates a new genre through the interpenetration of theology, history, and literature, developing its own — predominantly corporeal — rhetoric through which to textualize lives.

The dominant trait of the text is its overwhelming reference to bodies and body parts. The preface is constituted through the incessant repetition of bodily parts: "la main," "le corps," "des coeurs et des yeux," "les yeux," "les cheveux," "la bouche," "le coeur ... le coeur." (p. 18, vv. 325-30)[1] Indeed, everything is anthropomorphized in this text and possesses a body: "Dieu .../ Met ses mains au devant de ses yeux en courroux/Sa barbe et ses cheveux de fureur hérissent,/Les sourcils de son front en rides s'enfoncerent,/Ses yeux changés en feu .../Son sein enflé de vent .../Il prit au poing.../Courba son chef dolent.../Il croisa ses deux bras.../Son coeur ne peut plus faire avec le monde treve/...d'un pied depité refrappant." (pp. 149-50, vv. 1390-1415) God's body is described anatomically, the earth is spoken of as possessing a body ("terre, qui sur ton dos..." p. 194, v. 285), the body of the Church is a recurrent motif ("en Tes membres [les Dieux de la terre] te font une insolente guerre" p. 93, v. 90), the book has a body and acts like a body, and d'Aubigné writes his own body into his text as well. His book begins as a product of a resurrection, thus announcing at the very onset the effect of resuscitation d'Aubigné intends the *Tragiques* to wield: "Va livre, tu n'es que trop beau/Pour estre né dans le tombeau." (p. 11 ) And, indeed, the book is spoken of corporeally; it is "mon enfant," who "allaicte," who wears "ta robe," who experiences emotions such as "honte [et] peur," who is anatomically depicted: "ton front." (p. 26)

Unlike other martyrologists such as Crespin and Foxe, d'Aubigné does not lament the dissolution of the body; rather, he exalts it and revels in it, painstakingly recording the occasions of its torture. For it is in the torture scene that the body, scarred and vilified, is ultimately exalted. The more the body is destroyed, the stronger the spirit becomes. D'Aubigné uses passive formulations to describe the situation of the body, but employs exclusively active verbs when speaking of the spirit: "le corps fut emporté des prisons comme mort,/ Les membres defaillans, l'esprit devint plus fort." (p. 121, vv. 183-4) The inanition of the broken body is contrasted with the vitality of the spirit: "Du lict elle instruisit et consola ses freres/

Du discours animé de ses douces misères." (p. 121, vv. 185-6). For d'Aubigné, the body was expressly fashioned in order to be tortured so that the word might be spoken through it.    It is therefore necessary that his textual body imitate and experience the trials from which it is derived. The paper on which *Les Tragiques* is written seems to suffer a wounding: it is broken, torn, torn away ("je desrobay de derrière  les coffres et dessous les armoires les paperasses enrottees et deschirees desquelles j'ay arraché ce que vous verrez." p. 4) Yet nonetheless those mutilated fragments come together to form a textual body that articulates the confessional word.   "Tirer," a key word in the text, expresses d'Aubigné's attitude toward the body; his bodies are "tirés" in a joint image of birth and death; they are "arrachés" limb by limb, but in so doing are actually subtracted from spiritual death: physical death is not final for d'Aubigné, and pain is only a medium for the expression of the power of the word.[2] As in the treatment of the other Protestant martyrologists, the body is not important in and of itself, but rather in two regards, both revealed through torture. First, the body is important because it is an opened space[3]: "Faisoit une dispute aux playes du martyr/De l'eau qui veut entrer, du sang qui veut sortir." (p. 165, vv. 591-2); "quelques uns vont reperçant les corps/Où les esprits et coeurs ont des liens trop forts/ Ces fendans ..." (pp. 165-6, vv. 635-37). The body constitutes a zone which must be traversed.   It is an arena of testing, a preliminary passage which must be entered to find the way to the Word.

Secondly, the body of the martyr acts as a model for those who read of its ordeal.   This is not a model in the sense of an hagiographic exemplum: it is not meant to be copied through a re-representation, in a visual sense, of its configuration or circumstances. Rather, the word it speaks will cause the conformity of the reader or hearer to the model. Unlike the lives of saints, in which individual saints are offered up for veneration, God himself is the focus:  the martyrs "ne sont pour grandeur,/Mais pour un rare exemple,/Rare exemple de Dieu." (pp. 119-120, vv.  115-122). And, unlike the hagiographies, these are exempla not of how to act; these are not static depictions to be imitated. Instead, the reading of the martyrs' fate and confession provokes a modelling phenomenon which is more like a process of assimilation into the

Godhead, one energized by the enunciation of the word torn from the suffering body. In this regard, the motif of separation is not one that engenders dissolution, but rather one which causes a new creation. Liberation of the soul from the body is to be desired, and creates union with God, the ability to pronounce the salvific word: "ils présentèrent à Dieu, mil ames despouillées/De leur corps." (p. 94, vv. 119). Yet, disembodied, their voices remain: "Qui, libres au sortir des ongles des bourreaux,/Toutes blanches au feu volent avec les flammes,/Pures dans les cieux purs, le beau pays des ames,/Passent l'ether, le feu .../Avec elles voloyent, comme troupes de vents,/Les prières, les cris, et les pleurs des vivants." (p. 94, vv. 119-201).

### The Speech of the Spirit

In order for the word to be spoken, it is necessary for the body to be broken. *Les Tragiques* is structured on a pile of bodily fragments constantly named throughout the text. Bones and limbs heap up as in a charnel house, but paradoxically the prevailing impression, despite the emphasis on death, is one of life. It is the life of the spirit which its stressed. It is always the speaking spirit ("l'esprit distributeur des langues" p. 133, v. 693), and the spirit which is enabled its speech through the demolition of the body. The torture enacted on the body possesses unprecedented powers of transformation. The suffering body surpasses itself in and through speech. Thus, the caged, tormented body of a prisoner is transformed into a preacher: the admonitory image of punishment for heresy which the Catholics had attempted to construct is thereby reversed into word which denounces that attempt: "Tesmoin deux ans six mois qu'en chaire si hautaine,/Le prescheur effraya ses juges de sa peine./De vers continuels, joyeux, il louoit Dieu,/Sa voix forte preschoit .../Des pures veritez sortoient de cette cage." (p. 126, vv. 406-410) Not only does the power of the word use and transform the pain of the body, but also the Protestant text denounces the Catholic image, a dichotomy typical of d'Aubigné's polemic (as well as that of other martyrologists such as de Bèze and Crespin). The Catholic monstrance is neglected as the crowd attends to the "preacher's" words: "Mais surtout on oyoit ses exhortations/Quand l'idole passoit en ses processions/Sous les pieds de son throne, et le peuple prophane,/Trembl[aient] à ceste voix plus qu'à la tramontane." (p. 127, vv. 411-414). The power of the word is related to the wind of the spirit, the Paraclete. Torture enables, rather than stifles, the confessional word: "pour l'esprit qui s'explique en des langues de feu.../Les paroles de feu sortirent de leur bouche." (p. 128, vv. 499-510). Language is thus the essential tie between God and the martyr. It sustains the martyr during his ordeal, and it constantly reminds him and those witnessing his torture of his affiliation with Christ: "C'est Dieu qui point ne laisse au milieu des tourments/Ceux qui souffrent pour lui: les cieux, les elements/Sont serfs de cettuy-là .. a ouy le langage/Du psaumier d'Avignon." (p. 126, vv. 391-4). Torture also produces text. Just as Crespin's confessors wrote in their own blood when ink was lacking, d'Aubigné's martyrs write the triumphant text of God's truth with the blood issuing from their wounds: "Chaque goutte de sang que le vent fit voller/Porta le nom de Dieu et aux coeurs vint parler,/Leurs regards violens engraverent leurs zeles/Aux coeurs des assistans." (p. 129, vv. 510-514). Thus, the written indictment the Catholics had rendered of the Protestant martyrs loses what Foucault would deem its social value to inhibit emulation; the *spectators'* bodies are marked with an acknowledgment of the martyrs' innocence. The bodies of the spectators are altered by the faith of the confessors: "Ce peuple pour ouir ces choses eut oreilles,/Mais n'eut pour l'accuser de langue." (p. 145, vv. 1201-02) They are deprived of their power to condemn through speech.

Innumerable similar depictions of the image surpassed by the text, the body's torture redeemed by the word, are scattered throughout *Les tragiques.* They are accompanied by the recurrent motif of the sowing of the seed, a theme d'Aubigné borrows from the Gospel. He here explicitly likens the martyrs' broken bodies to the seeds which must be scattered in their earthen grave in order to germinate for the harvest. The text is sown with these references, which the reader must then gather to create the textual harvest of Protestant redemption, just as d'Aubigné himself has collected them: "si serez vous, par moi, vers boutons amassez/Encor esclorrez-vous, fleurs." (p. 146, vv. 1228-29). The act of reading is thus an act of re-collecting ("les Anges diligens vont ramasser nos cendres/Les quatre parts du monde, de la terre, et la mer,/Rendront compte des morts ..." p. 106, vv. 670-71) so as to render an accounting. D'Aubigné shows in this manner that, when the Catholics believe they destroy the martyrs' bodies by attacking them and dismembering them, they are in fact, unbeknownst to them, furthering the word of the Lord. They are the paradoxical planters of the future Protestant harvest. "Que d'un champ tout foullé la face dissipee,/Dont les riches espics tous meurs et jaunissans/Languissent ... /Quelques espics levés .../Prennent vie en la mort .../Se gardent au printemps .../Pour resemer l'Eglise, encore quelques graines/Armés d'afflictions, graines que les mains divines/ Feront naistre.../Moisson de grand espoir:  car c'est moisson de Dieu/Qui la fera renoistre en son temps, en son lieu." (p. 168, vv. 722-44). For d'Aubigné, the body of the martyr acts as the hull of the seed: it is the container of the word which is released and activated by the devastation of the body :  "ceux qui portent de Christ en leurs membres la croix." (p. 106, vv. 635). This sort of process exists in Crespin's *Histoire des martyrs*, where the reference is to incense which must be pulverized and set aflame in order to be effective.[4] D'Aubigné speaks of a similar necessity of destruction in order to give life: "les cendres des bruslez sont precieuses graines/Qui, d'après les hyvers noirs d'orages et de pleurs,/Ouvrent au doux printemps d'un million de fleurs,/La baume salutaire." (p. 106, vv. 654-57). Ironically, through the dispersal of the body parts, more power actually accrues to the martyr (just as Catholics fractured saints' bodies to gain numerous body parts for objects of worship). The body of the martyr occupies a wider, more vast space through the presence of its components. "Leurs cendres, qu'on jetta au vent, en l'air, en l'eau/Profiterent bien plus que le puant monceau/Des charognes des grands que, morts, on emprisonne,/ Dans un marbr' ouvrage: le vent leger nous donne/De ces graines partout." (p. 118, vv. 61-71)[5] Their non-containment, their dispersal not into an artificial tomb but into the bed of nature (and the text d'Aubigné writes) enables their eventual resuscitation and underscores the potency they possess. They fertilize the hearts of the listeners, readers and fellow faithful with the seeds of their examples: "les pauvres de Lyon avoyent mis leur semence sur les peuples d'Alby; l'invincible constance des Albigeois s'espandit par l'Europe..." (p. 118, vv. 73-75) The Albigeois are almost fecundated, overshadowed ("mis leur semence sur") by the martyrs' example. Stylistically, the semi-colon here shows the relationship of imitator to model. D'Aubigné sows dismembered body parts like so many seeds he expects to harvest. "Vous, Gastine et Croquet, sortez de vos tombeaux/Icy je planteray vos chefs." (p. 134, vv. 719-20).

## "Esmouvoir" and Election

D'Aubigné's *Les tragiques* is not, on first view, a martyrology like Crespin's and Foxe's. It contains a capsulated history of the wars of religion from a Protestant perspective, and each of its seven books describes the effect of the wars on the persecuted. However, underlying any other developments is d'Aubigné's obsession with *making sense* of the devastated Protestant body. In each book of *Les tragiques* can be found references to Protestant martyrs. Most particularly the books of "Feux" and "Fers" in the *tragiques* develop anecdotes of martyrdoms. In most cases, these are d'Aubigné's own reworkings of material he borrows from Crespin's *Histoire des martyrs*. But the manner in which he deals with the data he borrows is quite different from Crespin's treatment. First, *Les tragiques* does not pretend to be comprehensive or encyclopedic, as do *Icones* and the *Histoire des martyrs*. D'Aubigné's hallmark distinguishing him from the other Protestant martyrologists is that of selectivity or choice. He demonstrates great concern over how to glean out those materials best suited to his ends. "Ma conscience en face .../... me prend la main en disant: 'Mais comment/De tant de dons de Dieu ton foible entendement/ Veut-il faire le choix? Oses-tu bien eslire/Quelques martyrs choisis .../et laisser à l'oubli comme moins valeureux...'" (p. 117, vv. 25-32). His ultimate criterion is that of "esmouvoir." D'Aubigné states his aim in the preface: his book is not a didactic or encyclopedic compilation; rather, he means through it to bestir the emotions, to move the body of the reader to react to, the bodies therein contained: "nous sommes ennuyés de livres qui enseignent; donnez-nous en pour esmouvoir." (4) He must select the material most likely to move and touch the reader, so best as to elicit a response. This is why his account is more explicitly literary than the other Protestant martyrologies. It is carefully crafted by the choice of its author to rule out any eventual choice on the part of the reader. While Foxe and Crespin present their readers with selections and invite them to judge for themselves, d'Aubigné mandates the response he desires, and ensures that he will obtain that response by only using material designed to provoke it. In this regard, *Les tragiques* is a text about election. It guarantees that those martyrs incorporated in it—and that includes d'Aubigné himself who poses as an additional martyr in the text—shall be saved. The limited number of martyrs mentioned in *Les tragiques* —as opposed to the countless cases documented by Crespin and Foxe—further attests to the role of models that they fill for the reader. They are not only "tesmoins" to the truth through the torture they experience; they are also representatives, for those who read the text, of the fulfillment of the requirements for salvation. In the preface, d'Aubigné describes the position of his body in relation to the bodies of the oppressors: he uses a slingshot, like David against Goliath, to throw "cailloux blancs" at the heads of his persecutors. The "caillou blanc" is a symbol of election.[6] But it is also the by-product of cremation: the "ashes" of which he so poetically speaks are, in fact, charred pebbles, the remains of the martyrs' bones refined in their fiery ordeal. Thus, d'Aubigné uses his martyrs not only as exempla, but also as weapons: he figuratively hurls their remnants at those who sought to destroy them, using their remains to undo their persecutors. His book, that which he actually intends to throw at them, is composed of the fragments of the martyrs' bodies. These fragments possess a new potency due to their incorporation in the text.

Thus, while like Crespin, de Bèze and Foxe, d'Aubigné writes to enroll his martyrs on the lists of the saved ("je ne t'oublieray pas .../Je tireray ton nom de la nuict tenebreuse/Ton martyr secret, ton exemple caché/Sera par mes escrits des ombres arraché." p. 140, vv. 993-96), he also intends that the names he inscribes thereon will have a dynamic power. Writing becomes activist in *Les tragiques*. One way this can be seen is through an examination of the body parts d'Aubigné stresses. Unlike Crespin, de Bèze and Foxe, who speak most frequently of tongues and hearts, while these parts are mentioned in *Les tragiques,* d'Aubigné tends most to emphasize hands and fingers: those parts of the body which serve to write. D'Aubigné thereby underscores the significance of the body as eventual creator of text. Mary Stuart writes with her "main," her "doigt." (pp. 122-3) God writes with "le ferme doigt de Dieu." (p.

123, v. 281; also p. 128, v. 468; p. 143, v. 1110; p. 143, v. 1129). Thomas Bilnee writes his confession, then burns his own hand in a candle flame to prevent himself from writing a retraction (in a process modelled on Mucius Scaevola, the hero of antiquity, and one which thereby inscribes the modelling phenomenon on which the martyrological narrative is based in d'Aubigné. p. 124) While the Protestant hand and fingers are privileged in d'Aubigné's sight, linking them with God the author, the Catholic body is also described in the text, this time with punishment being meted out to the appropriate offending body part. In this example, Henri IV, about to abjure and become Catholic, is suitably rebuked: "Quand ta bouche renoncera/Ton Dieu, ton Dieu la percera/Punissant le membre coupable/Quand ton coeur, desloyal moqueur,/Comme elle sera punissable,/Alors Dieu percera ton coeur." (p. 18, vv. 325-30).

D'Aubigné's book offers a paradigm for salvation in which d'Aubigné himself participates. He offers himself up as a mutilated martyr, demonstrating that word issues from the wound. He positions himself among the martyrs of whom he speaks: "Condui mon oeuvre, ô Dieu, à ton nom, donne moy/Qu'entre tant de martyrs .../Je puisse..." (p. 117, vv. 19-22). D'Aubigné inscribes his own personal experience, as well as that of the martyrs, in his text, to an extent that clearly distinguishes him as the most self-conscious, and the most literarily-aware, of all the Protestant martyrologists. While Crespin refers to his martyrs who write using their own blood, d'Aubigné refers to himself, as creating text from a personal trauma that duplicates the torment undergone by the martyr: "Il y a trente-six ans et plus que cette oeuvre est fait [sic], assavoir aux guerres du septante et sept à Castel-Jaloux, où l'autheur... se tenant pour mort pour les playes receues en un grand combat, il traça comme pour testament cet ouvrage." (4) D'Aubigné assimilates himself to his martyrs, intending to be considered as one of them: "...les distinctions que j'apporte partout seront examinees par ceux que j'offense, surtout par l'inique Justice pour me faire déclairer criminel de lèse-majesté. Attendez ma mort qui ne peut être loin, et puis examinez mes labeurs." (3) His authorship is coextensive with his agony, as he inscribes himself: "au roolle des martyrs je diray en ce lieu,/ce que sur mon papier dicte l'Esprit de Dieu." (p. 113, vv. 955-67). D'Aubigné's description of his own "martyrdom" is modelled on those actual martyrdoms he relates in *Les tragiques*. The emphasis is on the treatment of the body, and the subsequent separation of body from soul: "parmi ces aspres temps, l'esprit ayant laissé/Aux assassins mon corps en divers lieux percé,/ Par l'Ange consolant mes ameres blessures." (pp. 178-79, vv. 1191-92). It is out of this torment that the scene of writing arises.

### Writing With The Body

Similarly, for the martyrs, torture produces text. Anne du Bourg writes his body into a sort of annotated text at his funeral pyre: "je ne fay qu'un *indice* à un plus gros ouvrage." (p. 131, v. 609). Gastine and Croquet create a pattern out of the circumstances of their death which others will decipher and follow: "tant de braves tesmoins dont la mort fut la vie.../Marchons sur leurs desseins ainsi que sur leurs pas." (p. 134, vv. 737-40). The edifying deaths of other martyrs are offered up to be read as inspirational tracts: "Du bureau, du tombeau, je releve une fille/De qui je ne diray le nom ni famille./Le père encor vivant, plein de graces de Dieu,/En pais estranger lira en quelque lieu/Quelle fut cette mort dont il forma la vie." (p. 140, vv. 998- 1001). A similar phenomenon is described in "Fers," wherein the martyrs in heaven are portrayed watching their successors read of, and emulate, their faith: "les peres contemployent l'admirable constance/De leur posterité qui, en tendre enfance,/Pressoyent les mesmes pas qu'ils leurs avoyent tracés." (p. 157, vv. 283-85) Other martyrs write with their blood; here, a young girl splotches the air with her blood, writing a testimony of the torture she has undergone, as well as that Truth to which she attests: "sa main gauche seigna/Entiere dans son sang innocent se baigna./En l'air elle hausse cette main degouttante." (p. 143, vv. 1059-60).[7] The word-play between "sang" and "seing," or personal seal, shows the intimate relationship between the body and writing. Others are written on by God, to confirm them in their confession. "A l'esprit separé de son corps/Christ luy donna sa marque." (p. 145, vv. 1176-77). Some martyrs receive inspiration and fortitude by reading either the statements of, or the stories about, predecessor martyrs. Two texts (the former, and the one d'Aubigné writes from the ordeal of the young woman who is here depicted as the martyr-to-be) thus figure the dialogue between two bodies, a corporeal intertextuality: "Cette-ci, en lisant avec fréquents soupirs/L'incroyable constance et l'effort des martyrs,/Doutoit la verité en mesurant la crainte:/L'esprit la visita et la crainte fut esteinte." (p. 128, vv. 479-82). We note that reading elicits a response by the body, just as d'Aubigné's text is meant to compel the reader's active response:  the "soupir" of the prospective martyr demonstrates her reaction. Mary Stuart writes her testimonial ("son livret pour faire testament," p. 122, v. 228) to be read by others; in an image of engraving, her body emblazons an indelible text: "ces doigts victorieux ne graverent ceci/En cire seulement, mais en l'esprit aussi." (p. 123, vv. 251-52). What the martyr loses in enduring torture and death, she confides in the textual product she creates, to perpetuate in a literary sense the body's existence. Mary Stuart uses her body as the final seal on her book: "Elle arrache ses mains et maigres et mesmes/Des cordes avec peine .../Puis donna son livret au garde de la Tour/Avec ces mots escrits, 'si l'ame deschargee/Du fardeau de la terre, au ciel demi changee/Prononce vérité sur le seuil du repos/Et lors que mon esprit pour le monde qu'il lasse/Desja vivant au ciel, tout plein de sa richesse,/Doit monstrer par la mort qu'il aime verité/Pren ce dernier present, seau de ma volonté/C'est ma main qui escrit ces dernieres paroles.'" (p. 122, vv. 227-241).  In addition, we hear in this passage, as in a refrain, the three elements d'Aubigné emphasizes in his martyrology:  torture, truth and text.  The body is always at the inception of the book for d'Aubigné. The embodied text speaks truth, for its human word is assumed into heaven and into the divine Word; the fire that burns Anne Askeuve "vole/Porter dedans le ciel et l'ame et la parole." (p. 122, v. 205) D'Aubigné inscribes the body of his book into the narration of what befalls the martyrs' bodies by referring to those particular chapters in *Les tragiques* which memorialize the martyrs.  "Autre cinq de Lyon, liez de mesme noeuds,/Ne furent point dessous par les *fers* et les *feux*" (p. 128, vv. 455-56); "on vint des *feux* aux *fers*; lors il s'en trouve peu/Qui vinssent du *fer* au *feu*." (p. 134, vv. 715-16).  And as d'Aubigné writes himself in among the martyrs through the medium of his text, he shows the body of his text in symbiotic relationship to his own.  He will perpetuate the martyrs' memory — make them live again.  Similarly, he will live eternally in his book: "encores vivrai-je par toy." (p. 11, v.7) Norris also writes the text of salvation in his blood. "...va le sentier estroit qui est jonché d'espines/...pieds nus.../sur ces tapis aigus ainsi jusqu'à sa place/A ceux qui le suvyront il a rougi la trace/ Vraye trace du ciel." (p. 120, vv. 135-145). Bleeding, he writes his *own* inscription on the place designated for his martyrdom. Both those persecutors who follow him, and successive victims who tread on the traces of his torture, must acknowledge and read and his marks.

## Catholic vs. Calvinist Reading

Key words such as "lire," "dessein," "traces" and "seing" reinforce the literary interpretation of the theological statement. The martyrs in heaven also *read* of what is to become of those who follow them: "... en l'histoire lisent..."; "dans le ciel, desguisé historien des terres,/Ils lisent..." (p. 158, vv. 323-24). The Angels act as writers and recorders of the texts that issue from the torture situation: "tout l'ordre des faits/Est si parfaictement par les Anges parfaits/Escrit, deduit, compté" (p. 158, vv. 313-15). The oscilla-tion between mention of the body and reference to a text is constant throughout *Les tragiques*. It functions to confer a convincing corporality on the text. And, finally, the reader reads the text of the martyr's body: "mon lecteur ... nous lisons après dans les effects ... le registre .. pour jamais engravee ... le registre saint." (pp. 179-180, vv. 1204-53). The appropriate reading act by the reader is caused to conform to the reading Protestants effect of Catholics in the text: they reinterpret that which the Catholics say, thereby opposing two different sorts of reading:[8] "Son visage luisit de nouvelle beauté/Quand l'arrest lui fut leu. Le bourreau présenté,/Deux qui l'accompagnoient furent pressez de tendre/ Leurs langues au couteau;/ ... disant .../'N'est-ce pas bien raison que les heureuses langues/ Qui parlent avec Dieu.../...quand tout le corps à Dieu se sacrifie/Sautent dessus l'autel pour la première hostie?'" (p. 128, vv. 495-98)[9] They rename their punishment, creating from it an occasion to transform their bodies into vehicles of God's truth. The Catholics, d'Aubigné asserts, are damned through incorrect reading. "Vous en avez chez vous une marque certaine/Dans vostre grand palais, où vous n'avez point leu.../Par un prophete ancien une histoire tracee/Ne se descouvrent plus qu'aux esprits advisez." (p. 107, vv. 682-89). Not only must the body be transformed into text, but only an informed reading will reactivate the body and generate the salvific power of the text.

The Protestant custom of tokens called the *mereaux* is illustrative of the manner in which d'Aubigné expects the martyrological narratives contained in *Les Tragiques* to function. These artifacts may also elucidate for us the relationship both of borrowing and of differentiation that exists between what I distinguish as the two separate genres of hagiography and martyrology. *Mereaux* were first employed by Catholics as *merallus* in the twelfth century. Ordinarily, they consisted an image on the verso and an inscription on the recto sides of a coin-like disc. They were accorded to pilgrims at pilgrimage sites to attest to the visitation of a holy place[10] and so functioned as do hagiographies in the sense first of dispersal and then of accumulation. When adopted by the Protestants, these token-like objects assumed a totally different function. They were distributed either to those believers who had led an upright moral life and who were therefore deemed fit to communicate at the holy table, or they were surreptitiously exhibited, in the palm of the hand of a travelling Calvinist, to fellow Calvinists in the new area in which he arrived, as a mark of identification. In this sense, the Calvinist hand carried on it a written message; the body was the locus for the displaying of the word, in a prefiguration of the way in which Protestant martyrs turned their bodies into sources for the utterance of the Word (e.g. Crespin's martyrs who wrote their confessions in blood) or in which Catholics attempted to annihilate the body of the Protestant by carving a punitive sentence into their flesh.

These *mereaux* were sometimes called *marques,* a term that is striking because it is one customarily employed in the sixteenth century as synonymous with *devise*.[11] The *devise* was a collection of images and short label intended to represent the essence of the person who had designed or commanded it. Thus, the Calvinist *mereaux* are profoundly linked with the existence and disposition of the body. In the first case, the surveillance of the body actually speaks for and confers legitimacy on the body, and in the third, the *mereaux* display the distinguishing marks of the individual. It is significant that the iconography of the *mereaux*[12] is altered when the Calvinists take it up: the image on the verso side, an exact representation (e.g. the portrait of the saint visited) becomes more allegorical or symbolic: the most common is that of the *berger,* the shepherd who represents, but is not himself *exactly,*[13] Christ, or the cup of wine which symbolically stands for Christ. Similarly, the type of inscription changes. The Catholic *mereaux* would note the place visited; the Protestant *mereaux* record the body of the church to which the traveller belonged (e.g. Bordeaux; l'église du désert) or inscribe a verse from Scripture on the recto side.[14]

This latter selection is particularly important, for it creates an emblem-like construction: the image on the front is associated with the writing on the back; they are interrelated and are meant to be jointly interpreted. Theodore de Bèze's *Icones* join body and word to create an emblematic text. D'Aubigné's text is emblem-like, but in a different way. He offers up images of himself, and quotations not always from Scripture but rather snippets and citations of his own previous works as authoritative. His body and word stand as witness and guarantor in the text to the bodies and words of the martyrs contained there. He offers his book as an itinerant or fugitive Calvinist would have shown his *mereaux,* as an authenticating mark, a token of effective communication between two men of like minds, in this case, he hopes, the author and the reader. The martyrological narratives in the *Tragiques* thus act, to some degree, as double *marques.* They attest to the martyr's authenticity ("O martyres aimez! ô douce affliction!/Perpetuelle marque à la sainte Sion,/Tesmoigne secret que l'Eglise en enfance/ Eut au front et au sein" (p. 204, vv. 703-707) as well as to that of d'Aubigné and his text. D'Aubigné is aware of the singularizing *marques* of the Calvinists; they are marked with the signs of their faith and of their election. The Catholics are also cognizant of the significance of these marks, and work always to obliterate them: "Mais du tableau de Tours la marque plus hideuse/Effaçoit les premiers .../Trois cens liés.../Les assomma, couplés/...Sans conoissance/De noms, erreurs et temps, marques et difference." (p. 165, vv. 605-618).

Text and body are inextricably linked. D'Aubigné's elaboration of his book, that is, his act of composition, is co-extensive with his life: "comme pour testament cest ouvrage, lequel encores quelques années après il [d'Aubigné] a peu polir et emplir." (4) The book will speak his name, as in a *devise* or *marque,* just as, symbiotically, his word energizes the book: "Quant à son nom, on n'exprime point les noms aux tableaux; il est temps que vous l'oyez par sa bouche, de laquelle vous n'aurez point de louanges servils, mais bien de libres et franches verités." (9) His "bouche" becomes the book. But the act of reading occurs with his anticipated death. His book is the product of an assemblage of fragments: the body, figured and dispersed in bits of written evidence, comes together in a text: "je desrobay de derrière les coffres et dessous les armoires les paperasses crottees et deschirees." (4) He links the parts of the corpus of the text as though aligning joints and bones, "comme des effects aux causes." (6) Like the martyrs, the disappearance or would-be annihilation of the body is not a reason to mourn, but rather to read, and through reading to resurrect the intentionality of the body.

### Mutilation and Monuments

The images of textual resurrection of the body employed in *Les tragiques* are complex and varied. Because d'Aubigné writes a self-consciously literary work[15] rather than a history[16] or an explicitly-avowed martyrology, he creates structures, or artistic constructions, from the broken bodies of the martyrs. In so doing, he redeems them from the mutilation and disfigurement visited on them by their tormentors, and exalts them as enduring monuments, the "new creations" for which the Gospel calls. The Catholics attempt to create an anti-monument, cannibalizing the remains of their victims: "Nous avons parmi nous cette gent cannibale,/Qui de son vif gibier le sang tout chaud avalle,/Qui, au commencement par un trou en la peau,/Succe, sans escorcher, le sang de son troupeau,/Puis acheve le reste, et de leurs mains fumantes,/Portent à leurs palais bras et mains innocentes,/Font leur chair de la chair des orphelins occis" (p. 95, vv. 195-204). The Catholics create an architecture of death out of life: "Et toy, Sens insensé, tu appris à la Seine,/Premier à s'engraisser de la substance humaine,/A faire sur les eaux un bastiment nouveau,/Presser un pont de corps: les premiers cheus dans l'eau/Les autres sur ceux-là; la mort ingénieuse/Froissoit de testes les testes" (p. 164, vv. 586-590). But d'Aubigné imitates God ("l'ouvrier parfaict de tous, cet artisan supresme/Tire de mort la vie..." p. 106, vv.) and reverses their attempt, creating an architecture of life from death: "Mais Dieu trouva l'estoffe et les durs fondemens,/Et la pierre commune à ces fiers bastimens/Les cendres des bruslez avoyent servi de sable/L'eau qui les destrempoit estoit du sang versé,/La chaux vive dont fut l'édifice enlacé/Qui blanchit ces tombeaux et les salles si belles/C'est le meslange cher de nos tristes moelles" (p. 95, vv. 179-186). The "chair" devoured by the Catholic cannibals is "cher" to God; the body is lifted out of its state of mere physicality and endowed with significant spiritual attributes. The Catholics destroy or reconfigure in an unrecognizable form the bodies of their victims: "Des tais des condamnez et coulpables sans coulpes/Ils parent leurs buffets et font tourner leurs coupes/Des os plus blancs et nets leurs meubles marquetz/Resjouissent leurs yeux de fines cruautez./Ils hument à longs traicts dans leurs couppes dorees/Suc, laict, sang et sueur des veuves esplorees;/...Sur des matras enflez du poil des orphelins..." (P. 96, vv. 209-19). They put the body parts to elaborate, artificial use, but God restores integrity and art, rather than artifice. The natural, bodily building God and d'Aubigné create is contrasted with nefarious constructions: Babel, the papal palace, the halls of the Inquisition, "l'abregé d'enfer" (p. 103, v. 535). D'Aubigné, like God, restores coherence. In his textual constructions, he forms a permanent, appropriate artistic monument to the martyrs. He strenuously disavows stylistic reworking[17] to distinguish himself from the false, deforming process the Catholics inflict on the Calvinists. His plain style is like that of God, the artisan: his text displays an integral, organic product. The "living stones" of which the Gospel speaks are the reunited skeletons of the martyrs who, through their use as building materials in a new construction through art, live again.

Bodily parts are reintegrated through d'Aubigné's literary endeavor, but always in a sense faithful to those bodies: they are not distorted, or put to unnatural uses. Similarly, d'Aubigné always maintains a hierarchy between image and word in his text. Like Crespin and Foxe, he inevitably privileges the latter over the former, and usually associates imaged fabrications with Catholic expression. Catholic pronouncements are illusory; they lack substance and truth. They do not write authoritative word, but merely display deceitful paintings of what they wish reality to be: "[ils] ne donnent le ciel ne l'enfer qu'en peinctures" (p. 104, v.

554). Images and painting contrast negatively with the raw, unadorned word: "à leur dieu de papier il faut un appareil/De paradis, d'enfer et démons tout pareil/L'idolâtre qui fait son salut en image/Par images anime et retient son courage/Mais l'idole n'a peu le fidelle troubler" (p. 104, vv. 555-59). Images are as unenduring as smoke. The Catholic attempt to portray through images their perception of the Protestants as heretical perishes in the same flames as the martyr, thereby confirming the untruth of the painting: "Hus, Hierosme et Prague ... bien cognus.../Des tesmoins que Sodome a trouvés par les rues/Couronnez de papier, de gloire couronnés/Par le siege qui a d'or mitres et ornés/Ceux qui n'estoyent pasteurs qu'en papier et en titres/Et aux evesques d'or fait de papier les mitres/Leurs cendres qu'on jetta..." (p. 118, vv. 61-71). The body thereby acts for d'Aubigné as that battleground on which the ultimate struggle between word and image is enacted, with the stakes being eternal life. The Catholic layer images over the Calvinist bodies, seeking thereby to distort them and conform them to their own sense: "...les rangs des condamnez, de sambenits couverts,/Portaient les diables peints.../Les hommes sur leurs corps desployent leurs injures..." (p. 105, vv. 552-54). We note that the author associates the Catholics, through images, with the images they paste onto Protestant bodies, cleverly condemning them to the very fate they had wished on their victims. "Enfin venoit ... le grand estendard rouge de la sacrée inquisition, portant d'un costé en borderie le nom, le pourtraict et les armes du pape sixte quatriesme, et de l'autre les images et noms de Ferdinand et d'Ysabelle." (p. 104) This is again a sort of *devise,* parading the names and images of the Pope, the King and Queen as they triumphantly enter the *auto-da-fé.* But their proximity with the images placed on the martyrs links the two in a similar destiny. D'Aubigné leaves them to their fate. They had been forced to march in procession to the pyre, bearing images "du manteau, du roseau et couronne d'espines..." (p. 105, v. 553) of Christ. D'Aubigné contrasts these false, death-dealing images with God's truthful banner: "lors que le fils de Dieu sa banniere y planta/Nous sommes des premiers images veritables" (p. 148, vv. 1332-33). The book "Feux" opens with a reversal of that malefic parade, with the elect processing and wearing Christ's insignia as marks not of punishment but of redemption: "marcher de rang ... au roolle des

esleus ... l'enseigne d'Israel" (p. 117, v. 2). Their bodies, though
burned, have not been utterly destroyed but rather purified,
rendered clear; the damning inscription of the Catholics has been
erased: "les feux qui vous brusloyent vous ont rendus candides" (p.
117, v. 14). Although the Catholics fractured and dissipated the
body, God has taken it up: "Ils dissipent les os, les tendons et les
veines/Mais ils ne touchent point à l'âme par les geines./La foy
demeure ferme et le secours de Dieu/Mit les tourmens à part, le
corps en autre lieu" (p. 121, vv. 177-80). This salvific subtraction
of the body is mimed syntactically by the placement of the comma,
which separates the body from the torture it suffered ("les
tourmens à part, le corps en autre lieu"). Isabella and Ferdinand
are depicted on an Inquisition banner which d'Aubigné deems
"l'infernal estendart;" their portrayal there confirms their sinful
nature. The paintings and images the Catholics created are viewed
by God, who then reverses them into word: "Dieu vid en mesme
temps/Car le prompt changement/De cent lieux ne luy est qu'un
moment/Deux rares cruautez/...Deux precieux tableaux,/Deux
spectacles piteux" (p. 120, vv. 147-153). He makes their images
into text as he reads them into the *rota* of the elect: "rendront
compte des morts qui lui plaira nommer" (p. 106, vv. 671-72). God
makes an accounting of the Protestants, then compels the
Catholics to try to make an accounting of themselves: "Dites vrai,
c'est à Dieu que compte vous rendez" (pp. 114-15, vv. 1000-14).
Some of the martyrs prefigure this divine process. Anne du Bourg,
for instance, verbally reverses the pain visited onto his body on to
that of his persecutors, detailing each body part in which they will
suffer. His voice negates the images they create, as he redefines
them in his own terms:

> "vous n'estes compagnons, plus juges, mais bourreaux,/Car en nous
> ordonnans tant de tourmens nouveaux/Vous prestez vostre *voix*; vostre voix
> inhumaine/Souffre peine en donnant la sentence de peine,/Comme, à
> l'exécuteur le *coeur* s'oppose en vain/Au coup forcé qui sont de l'exécrable
> *main*,/Sur le seige du droict vos *faces* sont/Quand, transies demi-vifs, il faut
> que vous ostiez les vies/Qui seules vivent bien: je pren tesmoins vos
> *coeurs*/Qui de la conscience ont ressenti les pleurs;/Mais ce pleur vous
> tourmente et vous est inutile" (p. 130, vv. 555-65; my emphasis).

The word, produced by the voice, is identified by du Bourg as
the seat of being; the Catholics suffer through the indictment they

have uttered. Contrarily, they seek to silence the speech of those whom they persecute. Silenced themselves, they are forced to hear the Word of God spoken by the martyrs' bodily parts even when their tongues have been torn out: "Dieu à ses tesmoins a donné maintesfois/ La langue estant couppee, une celeste voix"(p. 106, vv. 644- 52); "s'ils vous ostent vos yeux, vos esprits verront Dieu;/Vostre langue s'en va: le coeur parle en son lieu" (p. 137, vv. 847-48).

## Torture Into Text

While d'Aubigné's ultimate aim is to enable these voices to speak again in the text, we note nevertheless a striking attention to the details of the body in the torture process. He observes, for instance, "Par trente jours entiers ces filles, deschirees,/De verges et fers chauds demeurent asseurees;/La nuict on les espie, et leurs sanglantes mains/Jointes tendoyent au ciel: ces proches inhumains/ Dessus ces tendres corps impiteux s'endurcirent" (p. 141, vv. 1013-1022). At the same time as he denies the body as far less significant than the soul, there is nevertheless a sort of perverse intimate solicitude for the accidents of the body. His aim seems to be to make the reader feel the pain, and then surpass it through reading. The medieval and Renaissance genre of the *blason*, in which the loved one's body is deconstructed through minutious enumeration and through the obsessive focus on one body part separated from the rest of the body, is here a helpful model. D'Aubigné lovingly rehearses each wounded bodily component, turning torture into text, polemic into literature.[18] He thereby reworks images of pain into statements of glory: "Tu as ici rang, ô invincible Haux!/Qui pour avoir promis de tenir les bras hauts/Dans le milieu du feu, si du feu la puissance/Faisoit place à ton zèle et à ta souvenance:/Sa face estoit bruslee, et les cordes des bras/En cendres et charbons estoit cheutes en bas/Quand Haux en octroyant aux freres leurs requeste/Des os qui furent bras firent couronne à sa teste" (P. 120, vv. 127-34). By identifying the martyr's name ("Haux") with the significant placement of his arms (that is, "hauts"), d'Aubigné makes the body speak its own testimony and salvation: the body is consonant with the intention of its inhabitor, and through its positioning makes its statement. The rearranged bones of the arm create a "couronne" of glory, just as the reordered fragments of the martyrs' testimonials are exalted in the martyrological narratives of *Les tragiques*.

Other strange and wonderful occurrences befall the body parts enumerated in the text. Ann Askeuve's heart is left untouched by the flames that devour the rest of her body. The text acts as its shield, reenacting the fire's impotence: "...le feu violent/Ne brusloit pas encore son coeur en la bruslant;/Il court, par ses costés, en fin, leger, il vole/Porter dedans le ciel et l'âme et la parole" (p. 122, vv. 203-5). What subsists after the devastation of the body is the word, which is then assumed into the divine Word. Gardiner's body is transformed into an altered substance, an adamantine corpus so that the sufferer is insensate, unaffected by torture. The text exalts this triumph: "le fer contre son coeur de ferme diamant .../On coupe sa main dextre,/il la porte à la bouche avec sa main senestre/La baise; l'autre poing luy est couppee soudain/Il met la bouche à bas et baise l'autre main" (p. 124, vv. 309-12). This careful geometry of self-reconstitution evidenced by Gardiner figures the elaborate network of textual resurrection found in *Les tragiques*.

The textual rehearsing of body parts by d'Aubigné repeats and reverses the Catholic program of progressive destruction of the body, always with the concern to forestall its potential speech: "...pour rompre leur voix". Here, the disembodied word prevails; the Protestant body is surpassed, its container cracked open and devastated so that the contained, confessional word may emerge[19]: "le vulgaire anime entreprend sur leur vie,/Perce de mille coups des fidelles les corps,/Les couvre de fagots: ceux qu'on tenoit pour morts/Quand le feu eut bruslé leurs cables, se leverent,/Et leurs poulmons bruslans pleins de feu, s'escrierent/Par deux fois: Christ! Christ! Et ce mot, bien sonné/Dans les costes, sans chair fit le peuple estonné" (p. 127, vv. 439-52). The body may also be a tool for the liberation of the soul. The image employed is corporeal: the martyr consciously sacrifices himself, taking his soul into his hands, out of its bodily cage, to deliberately set it free: "tiens ton âme en tes mains" (p. 138, v. 891).[20] The reliance on the body as a tool is relentlessly underscored in *Les tragiques*, for even when the soul has been liberated, it is still described in bodily terms as though to glorify the body of the martyr, from which it derives;

here, it is compared to a pilgrim: "on dit du pelerin, quand de son lict il bouge,/Qu'il veut le matin blanc, et avoir le soir rouge:/Vostre naissance, enfance, ont eu le matin blanc,/Vostre coucher heureux rougit en vostre sang" (p. 147, vv. 1273-76). The resurrected body of Christ, teaches Scripture, is in some measure altered. It has defeated death. It is glorified, and no longer corruptible. As the martyrs' bodies are discarded, they are made like Christ, while Death is personified, and possesses a human, corruptible body: death, now embodied, too shall see death. The body parts of Death are listed to stress his ephemeral being: "les ongles de la mort..." (p. 137, v. 859). Thus, the martyrs' truth occurs through the proof rendered by the body. Gastine and Croquet will confer substantiality on their confessional statement through a bodily guarantee: "Or, je voy qu'il est temps d'aller prouver par moy/Les propos de ma bouche; il est temps que je treuve/En ce corps bien heureux la pratique et l'espreuve" (p. 138, vv. 904-14). And through the pain of the body always emerges the validating word; the body is uplifted and transformed: "Cet enfant, non enfant, mais âme desjà saincte,/De quelque beau discours, de quelque belle plaine/Estonnoit tous les jours... (p. 143, vv. 1059-90). Indeed, it is only through suffering that the martyr can truly experience the one-ness with Christ to which she had, living, always aspired. God participates with her in her agony, supplementing her personal resolution with divine strength: "leurs membres delicats ont souffert en maint lieu/Le glaive et les fagots en donnant gloire à Dieu/Du Tout-Puissant la force, au coeur mesme des femmes,/Donna vaincre la mort et combattre les flammes" (p. 148, vv. 1310-14). The enunciation of the confessional word signals that moment at which the martyr's body takes on the lineaments of Christ. God's body is portrayed in detail, as the martyr's body conforms to it: "Et pour dernière voix elle dit gemissante:/'O Dieu pren-moy la main/...Dieu ne refusa point la main de cet enfant/Son oeil vid l'oeil mourant, le baissa triomphant,/Sa main luy prit la main, et sa dernière haleine,/Fuma au sein de Dieu qui, présent à sa peine,/Luy soustint le menton, l'esveilla de sa voix;/Il larmoya sur elle, il ferma de ses doigts/La bouche de louange achevant sa priere,/Baissant des mesmes doigts pour la fin la paupière" (p. 143, vv. 1059-90). The face of the martyr becomes the face of God, through an overlayering technique in which the latter is visible, like a tattoo in the skin, in and through the former: "quand la face de Dieu brilla dedans la sienne" (p. 147, v. 1282).

This overlayering process is one which, like other strategies in d'Aubigné and the other martyrological accounts, imitates with the intent to overturn Catholic procedure. We find in d'Aubigné the same powerful image of redemptive overlayering, one which reverses Catholic intention, as can be seen in other Protestant martyrologists, most notably Jean Crespin.[21]

> "Mais qu'est-ce que je voy? un chef qui s'entortille/Par des volans cheveux, autour d'une cheville/Du pont tragique, un mort qui semble encore beau/Ses cheveux, arrestant au premier precipice,/Levent le front en haut qui demande justice./Non, ce n'est pas ce poinct que le corps suspendu/... C'est un sein bien aimé, qui traine encore en vie, pour chere compaignie,/Aussi voy-je mener le mari, condamné,/Percé de trois poignards aussi tost qu'amené,/Et puis poussé en bas, où sa moitié pendue/Receut l'aide de luy qu'elle avoit attendue/: Car ce corps en tombant des deux bras l'empoigna,/Avec sa douce brise accouplé se baigna ... /Appren, homme de sang, et ne t'efforce point,/A dessunir les corps que le ciel a conjoint" (p. 172, vv. 901-919).

Here, the insistence on the body, and on its members, is even stronger than in Crespin, as each portion is listed, and the two halves of one body ("moitié", reminiscent of the Renaissance motif of the androgyne[22]) are rejoined. D'Aubigné, more than any of the other martyrologists, obsesses over the fractured body. His constant references to the joining of the martyr's body with God's body in mystical marriage are recalled here through the reunification of the married human couple. The Catholics who write their condemnation on the bodies of their victims as though to write over the Protestants' credo, are portrayed as layering their mistaken interpretation over the statements of the martyr, to distort, silence or erase the latter.[23] D'Aubigné depicts God writing over, or speaking over, this Catholic judgement in order to negate the Catholic effect. "L'esprit donna des voix/Aux muets pour parler, aux ignorants des langues,/Aux simples des raisons, des preuves, des harangues/Ne les fit que l'organe à prononcer les mots/Qui des docteurs du monde effaçoyent les propos" (pp. 147-48, vv. 1304-7).

Protestants in d'Aubigné's martyrological narratives thus attend to the body and reflect on the nature of imagery, but in ways opposed to the Catholic treatment of both. Protestants reverse the Catholic inscription on the body, incorporating the martyr's word into texts: d'Aubigné's, and God's. Protestants distrust imagery. They observe it, then move beyond it, in a process that works from seeing to hearing or reading. It is only in this manner that word, and Word, can be attended to. We have seen that Catholics create visual representations of the tortures they mute out to the Calvinists; in fact, the writing the Catholics trace on the martyr's body works in *Les tragiques* less to make of the martyr a text. Instead, it makes of him an artifact, and one distorted from its original being. God's vengeance on the Catholics is motivated by viewing, and abhorring, those paintings: "D'un autre part au ciel en spectacles nouveaux/Luisoyent les cruautés vives en leurs tableaux,/En tableaux eternels afin que l'ire esmeue/Du Tout-Puissant vengeur fume par telle veue..." (p. 163, vv. 539-42). Similarly, the martyrs already in heaven view visual depictions of the events on earth. These are created by the angels, to indict the Catholics: "Tels serviteurs de Dieu, peintres ingenieux,/Par ouvrage divin representoyent aux yeux/Des martyrs bien-heureux une autre saison pire/Que la saison des feux n'avoit fait le martyre./Et cela fut permis aux esprits triomphans/De voir l'estat piteux ou l'heur de leurs enfans" (p. 157, vv. 275-282). But the martyrs are not mere passive viewers; rather, they are active readers, and revisionist interpreters of Catholics' actions. They are models for d'Aubigné's intervention in the text, as well as for the reader's reaction to it. D'Aubigné, as we have noted, portrays his own martyrdom in the text.[24] He also depicts his own resurrection. He is assumed into the heavens where, himself reader of the portraits about which the text comments, he figures the manner in which they are to be read: "les spectacles passez qui tournoyent sur la droicte... (p. 179, v. 1209). He then is revivified and returns from his celestial tour. His "esprit" rejoins his "corps," which he finds anew, just as he recuperates the bodies of the martyrs. The reunification of spirit and body is referred to in vocabulary that mirrors the reconstitution of the androgyne, the joining of the murdered husband and wife, and the ultimate unity of the martyr with God. The key word "moitié" reappears, stressing that d'Aubigné does not reject the body. Instead, he seeks its reanimation in a new form, through its reunification with the soul in a textual resurrection: "Retourne à ta moitié [d'Aubigné]/...voilà ton corps sanglant et blesme/Recueilly à Talcy, sur une table seul/à qui on a donné pour suaire un linceul/Rapporte-luy la vie" (p. 184, vv. 1417-28). D'Aubigné's martyrdom and resurrection prepare the way for the resurrection of the martyrs. Unlike de Bèze, Foxe and Crespin, d'Aubigné does not merely allude to the resurrection or proffer assurances of it. Instead, using images to his own purposes, he vividly describes the resurrection of the body. "Vos pères sortiront des tombeaux effroyables,/Leurs images au moins paroistront venerables/A vos sens abattus, et vous verrez le sang/...Ces pères saisiront vos inutiles mains,/En disant: 'Vois-tu pas que tes mains fayneantes/ Lavent sous celles-là, qui de mon sang gouttantes,/Se purgent dessous toy et versent mon courroux/Sur ta vilaine peau, qui se lave dessous?'" (p. 218, vv. 117-24). The emphasis on the hands of the progeny of the "pères," in this case the Protestant reader d'Aubigné directs his text toward, indicates the need for further action. The activity toward which hands have been directed in *Les Tragiques* is that of writing. The reader is called upon to craft a text that will continue the confessional utterance of textual bodies contained in *Les Tragiques*.

The martyrdom of the body leads to the speaking of the word. D'Aubigné's recitation of those words, in his own literary framework, reactivates them as forces in their own right: as textual bodies. The Protestant body, for d'Aubigné, exists in and through texts; it is the substance of which texts are made. The resurrection of the body in the body of the text constructs a chain that links in to it the body of the reader.

The portraits show the persecutors rending bodies into disconnected parts. The jumbling of body parts works to overwhelm all discursive coherence; it is an obsessional, incantatory repetition of destruction which the text must counteract: "Farouche!.../Deschire le troupeau qui, humble, ne deffend/Sa vie que de cris: l'un perce, l'autre fend/L'estomach et le coeur et les mains et les testes/...recevans pour esbats/Des testes, jambes, bras et des corps mis à bas" (p. 164, vv. 550-68). The destruction of bodily integrity parallels the Catholic attempt to silence the word; they deconstruct the syntax of the body into unrelated verbal elements, sounds without sense which must be reassembled to speak again in d'Aubigné's text.

The rhetoric of Reformation life-writing which is developed in *Les Tragiques* is theologically tendentious. That is, the lives written about serve a purpose beyond biography:  in a reversal of the biblical formulation in which the Word became flesh, here the flesh becomes Word; the martyrs' lives point beyond their existence to the Divine. Yet the strategy of self-inscription whereby d'Aubigne writes himself into his text also points up another, less critically-acknowledged aspect of Reformation life-writing: in a heightened awareness of the self arises from a situation of extreme tension and ordeal; the self then speaks about itself as self, and not merely as a self subsumed into a larger, ideological system.

# Notes

1. Agrippa d'Aubigné, *Les tragiques,* in *Oeuvres,* ed. Henri Weber (NRF, 1969). All other references in the text are to this edition.

2. "Je veux tirer à part la constante Marie,/Qui, voyant en mespris le tombeau de sa vie/Et la terre et le coffre et les barres de fer/Où elle alloit le corps et non l'ame estoffer:/'C'est, ce dit-elle, ainsi que le beau grain d'eslite/Et s'enterre et se seme afin qu'il ressuscite'" (p. 129, vv. 527-34). In a sense, this reenactment of her death makes d'Aubigné's text both her tomb (through the image of the "tombeau") and the site of her election ("tirer à part") through his word.

3. The images are of piercing, of forcibly opening: "Quelques-uns vont reperçant les corps/Où les esprits et coeurs ont des liens trop forts:/Ces fendans..." (p. 165-66, vv. 635-37).

4. Jean Crespin, *Histoire des martyrs.* ed. D. Benoit. (Toulouse: Société des livres religieux. 1885-89).

5. Images of dispersal conjoin with images of spreading: ..."l'invincible constance des Albigeois, frappez de cent mille morts, s'espandit par l'Europe, et en peupla ses bords" (pp. 118-19, vv. 71-76).

6. We see this stylistic linking elsewhere. Here, Fricht, soon to be martyred, imitates the martyr Bainam: "Là on vid un Bainan qui de ses bras pressoit/Les fagots embrasez, qui mourant embrassoit/Les outils de sa mort, instruments de sa gloire.../Fricht après l'imita, quand sa main desliee/Fut au secours du feu; il print une poignee/De bois et la baiza, tant luy semblerent beau/Ces eschellons du ciel comm' ornements nouveaux" (p. 119, vv. 91-100).

   D'Aubigné also reverses the modelling process: the persecutors who defaced their victims are then, in turn, themselves marked with the indictment of their iniquity: "où les mains des ennemis de l'Eglise cachent le sang duquel elles sont tachees sous les presents." (5)

8. See Jean Crespin for the inclusion of two different types of readers.

9. See John Foxe, *Actes and Monuments* IV, 361, for the narration of a young man, mutilated, whose mother praises God, because she views it as the mark of Christ.

10. I owe this information to the Olga de Saint-Affrique, curator of the Musée du protestantisme in LaRochelle during a conversation in July, 1990.

11. Circa 1530, marque and devise had very similar senses. Marque is defined circa 1530 as "signe materiel, empreinte mise sur une chose pour la distinguer ...sceau...signet." (*Le petit Robert*, p. 1048).

12. This is also the case with the alterations Protestant emblem book writers effected in the traditional use of iconography. See Georgette de Montenay, *Emblesmes ou devises chrestiennes*. (Lyon: Marcorelle, 1571).

13. Léon Wencelius, *L'Esthétique de Calvin*. (Paris: Les Belles Lettres, 1937).

14. I am indebted to Dr. Olga de St.-Affrique, curator of the museum and library at the Musée du protestantisme, La Rochelle, for her insights and helpful comments on this subject.

15. See Catharine Randall Coats, *Subverting the System: d'Aubigné and Calvinism*. (Columbia, Missouri: The Sixteenth Century Studies Press, 1990), particularly Chapter One.

16. He will record all this in a neutral, historical account, the *Histoire universelle*, but he defers this project, for "quand mes fruicts seront meurs ... et en prose coucher les hauts faits de sa gloire:/ Alors ces heureux noms sans eslite et sans choix/Luiront en mes escrits" (p. 118, vv. 44-48). We have already noted the importance of the act of careful selection for the literary construction of *Les Tragiques*; here, the history is characterized by its compendious inclusive quality.

17. See d'Aubigné, "Avis au lecteur," pp. 5 and 7.

18. In the same way, some martyrs choose to interpret their death as a willingly-accepted self-sacrifice. They may then turn their agony to a constructive purpose, and mold their bodies into the vehicle for a confessional statement: "...disant.../N'est-ce pas bien raison que les heureuses langues/Quand tout le corps à Dieu se sacrifie ..." (p. 128, vv. 495-99).

19. The reference to the body as mere container or shelter is used throughout the text: "Ce corps est un logis par nous pris à louage/Que nous devons meubler d'un fort leger mesnage/Sans y clouer nos biens, car après le trespas,/Ce qui est attaché nous ne l'emportons pas/...L'esprit sans corps, par qui le corps bruslé, seiché/N'estoit plus sa maison, mais quelque tendre voile,/Comme un guerrier parfaict campant dessous la toile,/Qu'on menasse de feu ces corps desjà bruslés,/O combien sont les feux par ceux-là mesprisés" (p. 135, vv. 785-89).

20. The Catholics experience a contrary phenomenon, in which damnation is indicated by the fact that the vehicle of the body is *not* surpassed: "Vostre corps est entier, et l'ame est entamee" (p. 136, vv. 835-37).

21. Crespin 707.

22. On the androgyne, see among others, "The Other and the Same: The Image of the Hermaphrodite in Rabelais," in *Rewriting the Renaissance*, ed.

Margaret W. Ferguson, Maureen Quilligan and Nancy J. Vickers, University of Chicago Press, 1986: 145-158.

23. The Catholics try to change the configuration of the body: "On brusle tout premier et sa bouche et sa langue;/...Ils bruslent son visage, ils luy crevent les yeux/Pour chasser la pitié en le monstrant hideux.../Mais le ciel de sa place/Ne contempla jamais une plus claire face" (p. 145, vv. 1165-77).

24. "Moy, qui rallie ainsy les eschapés de mort/Pour prester voix et mains au Dieu de leur support/Qui chante à l'advenir leurs frayeurs et leurs peines/ ...me tairay- je des miennes?" (p. 179, vv. 194-97).

# Conclusion:
# Textualizing the Protestant Body

Protestant martyrologies are not exclusively theological documents. They are literary documents as well. So one of the primary preoccupations of the Protestant martyrologists is to elucidate the relationship between the bodies about which they write (the "matière" of their book) and the text in which these bodies are subsequently integrated. Body and book, representation and dialogue, image and word are common themes in the martyrological collections of Foxe, Crespin, de Bèze and d'Aubigné.

This intimate situation in which body and text find themselves implicates other bodies. The bodies of the martyrs are reconfigured through the reassemblage of fragments of their speech and/or written word in the text. The body of the martyrologist stands as guarantor for these bodies, as it, too, is represented within the work, sometimes itself under the *figura* of a martyr. And, finally, the body of the reader is called to respond, bodily, to those bodies of which she reads, thus creating the future body of a textual commentary on the original text.

The text — *textus,* meaning tissue or bodily matter — thus exists in an organic relationship to the bodies of which it speaks. Most specifically, as we see especially in the works of Crespin and d'Aubigné, the text is produced within a torture scenario. The heightened awareness of a body — its pain, its destruction, its reintegration and possible resurrection — derives for Calvinists from the embattled position in which the Reformed church finds itself in the sixteenth century. The Calvinist body is maimed and destroyed by its persecutors. Consequently, it loses its spatial identity and becomes an entity recuperable only through the phenomenon of time, or memory: that which one safeguards in a text. Thus, the Catholic perception of the body displayed in hagiographies, the body as a localized site for the revelation of immanence, undergoes a fundamental alteration.  The Calvinist martyrologists, intentionally or not, may be the first truly modern theorists about the meaning, form, sense and uses of the body. The question of how to represent the body is an accompanying concern.

Calvinists use the body not as a container, but rather as a vehicle, for an apprehension of the Divine. The Word displays itself on and in the body through a palimpsest phenomenon, structures of inscription (the negative Catholic sentence) and superscription (the Calvinist scriptural affirmation of eternal life against the sentence of death) layer themselves on the body.  The text is formed from the body; the body seals the Word, and the Word redeems the body. The body is written into language, and emerges, on the other side of description, as a resurrected body integrated into the divine Word.

In the process, a new manner of defining both authorship and readership emerge.  The Protestant author defines his authorship in relation to the bodies which people his text; his word exists in juxtaposition to theirs—whether it be to frame their speech (Crespin), to comment upon or interpret their speech (Foxe), to conjoin representations of their bodies with their speech in an emblematic pattern (de Bèze), or to claim the status of a martyr for himself and thereby exalt his writing as a scripture of the self (d'Aubigné).

In this attempt to extrapolate a Calvinist aesthetics from martyrological narratives, I have dealt with the accounts as literary texts.  The texts themselves call for such a treatment, through the evidence of self-conscious authorship, through a mingling of genres in the main narrative, through patterns of citation from other works which generate a form of dialogic intertextuality, and through constant reference to the act of writing. The act of literary composition—selection and arrangement of materials, authorial framing techniques, directives for the reader—exists always in juxtaposition with bodily parts. The text itself becomes a sentient, reactive and provocative body through the bodies contained in it. This does not occur through a process of absorption or ingestion, as in hagiographic accounts, however.  Rather, the Calvinist processing of the body is one of dissection and reconstitution.

John Foxe constitutes his *Actes and monuments of the martyrs* as an intercessory entity between author and reader, militant Catholic and vigilant Protestant. Through the creation of story-like accounts, he opens an area of free interaction of the reader with the book. He looks for the reader's reaction, and solicits a dynamic interchange. He poses as an autocommentator of his text, while also indicating to the reader ways in which the reader can bring her interpretive schema to bear on the *Actes*. Thus, the text itself is generated in a layered pattern that mimes the process of inscription, erasure, and redesignation that the Catholics and Protestants incessantly perform on the martyrs' bodies. The middle position Foxe occupies, and into which he invites his reader, is figured by the images in the text. These act as didactic intercessors, to render the *Actes* more accessible. The reader's role, therefore, is to aid the author in apprehending, describing and reconfiguring the Protestant body. For the Anglican Foxe, the bodies of author and reader are jointly legitimized and serve to substantiate the text in which they stand. Indeed, throughout the *Actes,* the body functions as a place-marker for the reader, alerting her to particularly significant passages about the body, in a sophisticated self-witnessing and self-authenticating structure that we see again in d'Aubigné's martyrological narratives.

Crespin reconstitutes the textual body through miming then reversing its disappearance: he incorporates fragments of the body's utterance in episodic fashion, just as members would have been severed from the body. In the *Histoire des martyrs,* it is clear that, because the body has been totally destroyed, the only possible recuperation of corporeal form is textual: the body reemerges as an utterly reconfigured being. Crespin confers weight on this new textual body by describing it in explicitly bodily ways: his vocabulary is drawn from the parts of the body, the position of the body and the agonies experienced by the body. In addition, Crespin derives the legitimation for his innovative textual construct from the martyrs themselves, who specifically speak of their bodies as sorts of confessional books intended to display God's Word. The book is coextensive with their lives, and they conceive of themselves, primarily, as writers. Crespin realigns body parts in an attempt to make sense of them, as d'Aubigné does in *Les tragiques*; this is a syntactical project, in which portions of bodies stand symbolically for fragments of sentences. Speech is thereby reactivated and embodied in the *Histoire des martyrs.*

De Bèze memorializes the martyrs through a form of what Frances Yates has dubbed the "memory theater": he incorporates paraphrases of the martyr's speech along with woodblock representations to form an emblematic configuration. However, his body finds itself always at the fringes of this structure, hemming it in, causing it to conform to *his* own word and sense. There thus exists a powerful tension between word and image in *Icones*, ultimately resolved in favor of the word, which figures de Bèze's ambivalence over the proper textual incorporation of the confessing body. Such questions may arise from de Bèze's rigorous Calvinist orthodoxy, ordinarily much more conformist than that of the other martyrologists. *Icones*, a text that struggles within itself due to the competition between de Bèze's own speech and that of the martyrs, rehearses this struggle both through the word-image patterning and through processes of autocommentary (the concluding section of emblems which is attached to, yet separate from, the main body of the work.) De Bèze in this manner indicates the necessity for interpretation of Calvinist bodies: they are not to be viewed, but rather *read*. De Bèze's own body is "encrypted" within *Icones*, but must be deciphered to determine its role: multiple representations, past and present, corporeal and literary, of de Bèze proliferate. As de Bèze's description of his own body is a verbal phenomenon, so too is the resurrection he figures of the Calvinist body: the text, and reading of the text, lead to salvation.

Torture tears the text out of the body in d'Aubigné's *Tragiques*. Referring incessantly to innumerable body parts, d'Aubigné demonstrates that torture is necessary in order that the textual resurrection of the body may occur. The manner in which the text is constituted itself imitates the torture scene: it is wrenched away, on torn and crumpled paper, from hands which would silence it. For d'Aubigné, the speaking body predominates, since language makes possible the communication with, and an ultimate union between, God and martyr. Language also makes possible the conformity of d'Aubigné's, and the reader's, bodies to that of the martyr. We are swayed through speech, then spoken into the roll call of salvation. D'Aubigné models a notion of corporeal intertextuality, in which martyrs influence martyrs-to-be, who pattern the position and reaction of their bodies on their predecessors just as, by reading the text, the reader assimilates herself into the modelled roles. The Calvinist body necessarily regains its existence in and through the text: similarly, for d'Aubigné, any legitimate existence for the reader must be attested in the textual theater.

The four Protestant martyrologists demonstrate a literary sensibility that is linked to their awareness of self as experienced in the bodies they inhabit and in the bodies they discuss. The body poses as the privileged site for textual development. It also functions as that entity in and through which Calvinist authorial self-consciousness arises. "Life-writing" and literary production truly coexist in the resurrected, transformed body of the martyr as text.

# Bibliography

Abraham, Nicholas and Maria Torok. *The Wolf Man's Magic Word.* trans. Nicholas Rand. Minneapolis: University of Minnesota Press, 1986.

Aigrain, René. *L'hagiographie: ses sources, ses méthodes, son histoire.* Paris: Bloud et Gay, 1953.

Bainton, Roland. *Women of the Reformation in France and England.* Boston: Beacon, 1973.

Boesch-Gajano, Sofia. *Agiographia altomedievale.* Bologna: il Mulino, 1976.

Brown, Elizabeth A. "Death and the Human Body in the Later Middle Ages: the Legislation of Boniface VII on the Division of the Corpse." *Viator* 12 (1981). 221-70.

Brown, Peter. *The Body and Society.* New York, Columbia University Press, 1988.

Brown, Peter. "The Rise and Function of the Holy Man in Late Antiquity." *Journal of Roman Studies* 61 (1971). 85-87.

Brown, Peter. *The Cult of the Saints.* Chicago: University of Chicago Press, 1981.

Brown, Peter. "The Saint as Exemplar in Late Antiquity." *Representations* 1.2 (Spring, 1983). 1-25.

Byman, Seymour. "Ritualistic Acts and Comupulsive Behavior: The Pattern of Tudor Martyrdoms." *American Historical Review* 83 (1978). 78-86.

Bynum, Caroline Walker. *Holy Feast and Holy Fast.* Berkeley: University of California Press, 1987.

Calvin, Jean. *Institution de la religion chrestienne.* Geneva, 1541.

Calvin, Jean. "Traité des reliques". *Three French Treatises.* ed. Francis Higman. London: Athlone, 1970.

Camporesi, Piero. *La Chair Impassible.* Flammarion, 1986.

Camporesi, Piero. *L'Officine des sens.* Hachette, 1989.

Camporesi, Piero. *L'Enfer ou le fantasme de l'hostie.* Hachette, 1989.

Christianson, Paul. *Reformers and Babylon: English Apocalyptic Visions from the Reformation to the Eve of the Civil War.* Toronto: University of Toronto Press, 1978.

Coats, Catharine Randall. "Dialectic and Literary Creation." *Neophilologus 72 (1988). 161-167.*

Coats, Catharine Randall. "The Devil's Phallus: Humanistic vs. Theological Notions in Béroalde de Verville and Agrippa d'Aubigné." *Stanford French Review* (Spring, 1989). 37-48.

Coats, Catharine Randall. *Subverting the System: d'Aubigné and Calvinism.* Missouri: Sixteenth Century Publishers, 1990.

D'Aubigné, Agrippa. *Les tragiques. Oeuvres complètes.* Henri Weber, ed. Paris: Gallimard, 1969.

D'Aubigné, Agrippa. *Histoire universelle.* vols. 1-3. André Tournon, ed. 1981.

de Bèze. *Icones ou les vrais portraits des hommes illustres.* Alain DuFour, ed. Geneva: Slatkine reprints, 1964.

de Bèze, Théodore. *Histoire ecclésiastique des églises réformées au royaume de France.* G. Baum and E. Cunitz, eds. vol.1. Nieuwkoop: B. de Graaf, 1974.

de Bèze, Théodore. *L'histoire de la vie et mort de Maistre Jean Calvin, avec le testament et dernière volonté dudit Calvin, et le catalogue des livres par luy composez.* Geneva, Perrin, 1564.

de Cazelles, Brigitte. *Le corps de sainteté.* Geneva: Droz, 1982.

de Certeau, Michel. *L'Ecriture de l'histoire.* Paris: Gallimard, 1975.

de Gaiffier, Bernard. "La légende des Actes des martyrs dans la prière liturgique en Occident." *Analecta Bollandiana* 72 (1954). 134-66.

de Gaiffier, Bernard. "De l'usage et la lecture du martyrologue, Témoignages antérieures au XI^e siècle." *Analecta Bollandiana* 79 (1961): 40-59.

Delaruelle, F. *Histoire du catholicisme en France.* vol. 2 Paris, 1960.

Delehaye, Henri. *Les origines du culte des martyrs.* Brussels: Desclée, 1912.

Delehaye, H. *Les Passions des martyrs et les genres littéraires.* Brussels, 1921.

Delehaye, H. "Les premiers libelli miraculorum." *Analecta Bollandiana* 43 (1925). 427-434.

Delehaye, H. "Les recueils antiques des miracles des saints." in *Analecta Bollandiana* 29 (1910). 5-85; 305-82.

Du Bois, Page. *Sowing the Body.* Chicago: University of Chicago Press, 1988.

Duval, Y. M. and Charles Pietri. "Membra Christi: Culte des martyrs et théologie de l'Eucharistie." *Revue des Etudes augustiniennes* 21 (1975). 289-301.

Feher, Michael, ed. *Fragments for a History of the Human Body,* parts I-III. Zone, 1990.

Felman, Shoshona. *Le scandale du corps parlant.* Paris: Seuil, 1982.

Finucane, Ronald. *Miracles and Pilgrims: Popular Belief in Medieval England.* London: Dent, 1977.

Foucault, Michel. *Discipline and Punish.* Alan Goldhammer, trans. New York: Columbia University Press, 1979.

Foxe, John. *The Acts and Monuments of the Martyrs.* New York: AMS Press, 1965.

Frutaz, A. P. "Storia e leggenda, valore dogmatico, significato spirituale del culto dei santi." *Testi e documenti di vita sacerdotale e di arte pastorale* 16 (1970). 404-40.

Gilmont, Jean-François. "La genèse du martyrologie d'Adrian van Haemstede." *Revue d'histoire ecclésiastique* 63 (1968). 379-414.

Grabar, A. *Martyrium. Recherches sur le culte des reliques et l'art chrétien.* vols. 1-3. 1943-46.

Halkin, Léon. "Hagiographie protestante." *Analecta Bollandiana* 68 (1950). 153-63.

Haller, William. *The Elect Nation: The Meaning and Relevance of Foxe's Book of Martyrs.* New York: Harper, 1963.

Hamman, A. "La Confession de la foi dans les premiers Actes des Martyrs." *Epektasis. Melanges patristiques offerts au cardinal Jean Daniélou.* Paris: Beauchesne, 1972. 99-105.

Hermann-Mascard, Nicole. *Les reliques des saints: Formation coûtumière d'un droit.* Paris: Klinckseick, 1975.

Jounel, P. "Le Culte des saints." A.-G. Martimort. *L'Eglise en prière: Introduction à la liturgie.* Paris: Tournai, 1961. 766-85.

Kitzinger, E. "The Cult of Images in the Age Before Iconoclasm." *Dumbarton Oak Papers* 7 (1954). 33-62.

Kolb, Robert. *For All the Saints.* Mercer University Press, 1989.

Krautheimer, Robert. "Mensa, coemeterium, martyrium." *Cahiers archologiques* 11 (1960). 15-40.

Kristeva, Julia. *Powers of Horror: An Essay on Abjection.* New York: Columbia University Press, 1982.

Lamont, William. *Godly Rule: Politics and Religion, 1603-1660.* London: Macmillan, 1969.

Leclercq, J. *L'Amour des lettres et le désir de Dieu.* Paris: les Editions du Cerf, 1957.

Loux, E. *Le Corps dans la société traditionnelle: pratiques et savoirs populaires.* Paris: Berger-Levrault, 1979.

Marrou, H.-I. "Le Dogme de la résurrection des corps." *Patristique et Humanisme,* par H.-I. Marrou. Paris: Seuil, 1976. 429-454.

Mathieu-Castellani, Gisèle. *Emblèmes de la mort.* Paris: Nizet, 1988.

Musurillo, H. *The Acts of the Christian Martyrs.* Oxford: Clarendon Press, 1972.

Olsen, V. Norskov. *John Foxe and the Elizabethan Church.* Berkeley: University of California Press, 1973.

Piaget, Arthur and Gabrielle Berthoud. *Notes sur le livre des martyrs de Jean Crespin.* Neufchastel, 1930.

Puolin, J.-C. "Les Saints dans la vie populaire au moyen age." Lacroix and Boglioni, eds. *Les religions populaires.* Quebec: Presses universitaires de Laval, 1972.

Raitt, Jill, ed. "Theodore Beza 1519-1605." *Shapers of Religious Traditions in Germany, Switzerland and Poland.* New Haven: Yale University Press, 1981.

Riddle, Donald. *The Martyrs: A Study in Social Control.* Chicago: University of Chicago Press, 1931.

Rosello, Mireille. "Jesus, Gilles, Jeanne." *Stanford French Review* 13. 81-95.

Russell, Daniel. *The Emblem and Device in Renaissance France.* Lexington, Kentucky: French Forum Publishers, 1986.

Sanday, Peggy Reeves. *Divine Hunger and Cannibal Monsters: Cannibalism as a Cultural System.* Cambridge: Cambridge University Press, 1991.

Saintyves, P. *En marge de la Légende dorée.* Paris: Nourry, 1930.

Saybolt, R. F. "The 'Legenda Aurea,' Bible and the 'Historia Scholastica.'" *Speculum* 21 (1946). 339-42.

Scarry, Elaine. *The Body in Pain.* Berkeley: University of California Press, 1985.

Scarry, Elaine, ed. *Literature and the Body.* Baltimore: Johns Hopkins University Press, 1986.

Sherman, James E. *The Nature of Martyrdom.* Paterson, New Jersey, 1942.

Simonetti, Marc. "Qualche osservazione a proposito dell'origine degli Atti dei martiri." *Revue des Etudes augustiniennes* 2 (1956): 106-23.

Thompson, Geraldine Vina. "Foxe's Book of Martyrs: A Literary Study." Ph. D. diss. University of Oregon, 1974.

Tricot-Royer, "L'Eglise et la mutilation du cadavre humain: décarnisation—dissection pour enseignement—embaumement—autopsie." *Revue médicale de Louvain* 22 (1935): 33-49.

Webber, Joan. *The Eloquent 'I'.* Madison: University of Wisconsin Press, 1968.

Welter, J.-Thomas. *L'Exemplum dans la littérature religieuse et didactique du Moyen Age.* Paris: E.H. Guittard, 1927.

White, Helen C. *Tudor Books of Saints and Martyrs.* University of Wisconsin Press, 1967.

Wilson, Stephen, ed. *Saints and Their Cults: Studies in Religious Sociology, Folklore and History.* Cambridge: Cambridge University Press, 1983.

Wooden, Warren. *John Foxe.* Boston: Twayne, 1983.

Yates, Frances. "Foxe as Propagandist." *Encounter* 27. 1966: 78-86.

## DATE DUE

| JAN 2 1996 | | | |
|---|---|---|---|
| | | | |
| | | | |
| | | | |
| | | | |
| | | | |
| | | | |
| | | | |
| | | | |
| | | | |
| | | | |
| | | | |
| | | | |
| | | | |
| | | | |
| | | | |
| | | | |